PRAISE FOR
The Unexpected Leader

"Sean has done a masterful job of delivering a powerful message in a delightful story. This parable helps us all become more aware of the importance of relationships and leadership in shaping the success of any team."
— *Cory Dobbs, Ed.D.*
President & Founder of
The Academy for Sport Leadership

"*The Unexpected Leader* is a phenomenal story that any coach or player can relate to. More importantly, it hammers home a fundamental list of practical ways to succeed on and off the court. I read it cover to cover in one sitting and thoroughly enjoyed it... you'll love *The Unexpected Leader!*"
— *Alan Stein*
www.StrongerTeam.com

"What a GREAT BOOK! After reading the first 5 pages I had to stop and go get my highlighter. *The Unexpected Leader* is a MUST READ for anyone in a leadership position. After reading it and sharing it with your team leader I promise you will be able to get your team rowing in the same direction towards a common goal."
— *Terry Fowler*
UNA Women's Head Basketball Coach

A note from the author...

Whether you have purchased this book or received it as a gift, I am excited for you to turn the page and congratulate you for reading this powerful story and furthering your development as a leader.

Rising to a position of leadership is both a choice and a journey, and to assist you I have provided a FREE printable Reader's Guide for you to download and refer to as you read the book.

To get your copy, simply visit my website at http://greatresultsteambuilding.net/theunexpected leader/

The file is available on the *The Unexpected Leader* book page – and I hope it will be helpful to you as a tool for recognizingand reflecting on the main points of this story.

In addition to the *The Unexpected Leader Reader's Guide*, you will find a number of team building resources, articles, and handouts on my site to help lead from where you are!

And if your organization is in need of an engaging speaker to share an inspiring message about building or being a part of a successful team, let's talk!

Lead your team,
Sean

SEAN GLAZE

The Unexpected Leader

HOW TO ACHIEVE
TEAM SUCCESS
WITHOUT A TITLE

TABLE OF CONTENTS

CHAPTER 1

THE MEETING

MORE THAN AN HOUR AFTER HIS TEAM'S first game of the New Year had ended, Matthew was alone in the team locker room still covered with a thin film of cool sweat. He sat on the concrete slab bench with his back to the row of lockers and his face buried in his hands, fingers spread reaching up high enough to dig into his forehead of dark straight hair.

His elbows rested on tired legs that would become increasingly sore tomorrow from his efforts.

The purple and gold number 22 Knights basketball jersey clung uncomfortably to his back, and he could feel warm salty droplets moving in slow rivulets down his fingers and his forearm to drip just in front of his shoes onto the dull white-tiled floor beneath him.

The Hebrews High School locker room was empty and quiet and the painted cinder block walls felt more hollow than ever – no laughter remained from the pre-season workouts and ribbing between players after practices or conditioning workouts. Instead of a place warmed by enthusiastic smiles and optimistic expectations, it now felt more like a morgue.

Hebrews was a small private school that had invited Matthew on an academic scholarship when his coach heard he was moving into the area. It had fewer students than every one of his opponents in region 4A, but it had nicer facilities and provided a quality education his father didn't have to pay for, which was important considering their situation.

As he sat there alone, Matthew realized he hadn't ever before noticed the fluorescent shadows cast on the floor by the metal lockers and exposed ceiling pipes, but now they seemed to curl and drape themselves around the entire room like thick gray vines of life-choking kudzu.

A scary thought flashed in bold letters onto the swirling maelstrom of thoughts in his mind that had for nearly 20 minutes been consumed with disappointment, self-doubt, anger, and enough blame to fill a dump truck. This was only their ninth game! At 3-6, they had nearly fifteen more times to leave the gym with this ache!

He heard the echo of old Coach Dudley's steps coming from his office down the back hallway of the gym toward the heavy door that stood between them.

The door creaked open and coach just yelled in to him "Time to go son. I'm locking up in five." Coach Norm Dudley's voice remained just as gray and depressing as the shadows on the floor and wall. He was obviously frustrated, too. But the thing about frustration is, Matthew thought, it feels like a maze. And it only gets worse the longer you wander around lost and upset.

They needed to find a way out, and some of the players had already started to blame Coach Dudley's offense or his long practices or his critical fits of yelling for their lack of success on the floor. Paul and Tommy had been muttering about it since tryouts. And now, even Matthew – who would never say it out loud – had begun to wonder if there was some validity to his teammates' criticisms.

Their confidence in the coach was the first thing that started to dwindle – fueled by an unwillingness of his teammates to accept responsibility and an overly enthusiastic willingness of parents to accept it as an excuse for their sons' poor performances. Support for Coach Dudley had all but disappeared. But the longer the players struggled and bickered inside this maze of frustration and losing, the easier it got to wave goodbye to confidence in themselves as well.

Time to get up, he thought. Got another one tomorrow...

He reached behind him and grabbed his bag – there was nobody left in the gym by now, and he could leave the locker room in his uniform instead of changing. He'd let the cold air outside dry his jersey on the walk home. He knew that coach would hang around for a while – so if he left now, there'd be no questions about him not having a ride home.

The gym was dark, and Matthew's chin hung low, his downcast eyes only able to see where his feet would fall next. His shoes felt heavy as he began to move slowly up the gymnasium steps, and he tried to clear his mind as he neared the top to turn toward the concession stand and leave the building.

As he climbed, he heard a man almost whisper from the landing above him.

"Tough to see where you're going with your head down, kiddo."

Matthew hadn't expected any fans to be there, and didn't recognize the voice at all. It was deep and raspy, but clear enough to break through the silence and startle him. He felt his jersey wrinkle up in sweaty clumps around his shoulder blades as he raised his face up to see a young bearded man standing in the bleachers above him.

The man who had spoken was standing above him and shared a warm, knowing smile. He wore jeans and a tan work shirt, clenching a broom in front of him with both hands. His hair was parted to the side, and he had a closely trimmed beard to match the thick, neatly-combed short, brown strands above it.

The light tan of his work shirt and brown hair seemed a matching ensemble, and as he addressed Matthew he began to remove his right hand from the broom he had been pushing through the now empty stands. It was the school custodian.

Matthew began to slow his ascent, and although the voice had sounded full of a concerned kindness, the young custodian's next action caused Matthew to abruptly stop.

Instead of reaching out to shake Matthew's hand, the custodian turned his once spread fingers into a clenched right fist. His lips and jaw then tightened into a steely-focused look of intensity, and Matthew found himself completely paralyzed with surprise at the change in the janitor's demeanor.

The janitor stared intently at the fist he had made, shaking it slowly in front of his tan shirt, between himself and Matthew's confused stare.

The clenched fist then moved forward and back, until the custodian was furiously shaking it into a silent but intense crescendo.

Just as Matthew was growing uncomfortable, the bearded man with the broom stopped and smiled again. "You're one of the team's leaders, right?"

Matthew replied with apprehension – "yeah..."

The janitor's smile broadened and his eyes glowed again with warmth. "That's your answer, then..."

Matthew didn't understand.

"It's not what you want, but how hard and how long you are willing to work for it, especially through tough times!"

Matthew just stared blankly at him, incredulous.

The gym was empty – quiet and dark. His legs were still wobbly from exertion, his wet uniform was getting more uncomfortable, and he was beginning to hope that Coach would walk out so he didn't feel so alone with this guy who might be a complete weirdo.

"Thanks, sir. But I gotta go"

"You know, I'm a bit of a coach myself. Had a few guys that I helped a while back win over a huge following – they went on to become all-stars, too."

He reached back down, eyes following his hand as he wrapped it firmly around the broom again. "I bet you're pretty frustrated tonight. Feel like everything's going into the sewer?"

Matthew stayed quiet, but followed him as he picked the broom up and turned to move toward the gym exit doors. "Well, that frustration's understandable. But I can help you and your teammates out of that maze if you're willing to listen..."

Matthew stopped moving – froze himself in front of the closed concession stand window and looked up at the tall, brown haired man in front of him. "What did you just say?"

"You can be a leader of men, Matthew. It doesn't matter where you're from or what you've done in the past. Your success will always be based on your own merits, and measured by how willing you are to follow good advice."

The janitor pushed open one of the doors and cold air rushed in at them. He was holding it open for Matthew, and his head nodded at the parking lot.

"Enjoy your walk home, kiddo. If you want to talk more, I'll be around."

Nothing else was said – but Matthew moved through the doorway, as if in a trance, and wondered, as he trudged into the night, about the weird meeting, what the janitor had said to him, and how he could have known about that maze image he mentioned...

CHAPTER 2

THE MORNING AFTER

THE FROST ON HIS BEDROOM WINDOW WAS a cruel reminder that it would be another cold walk back in the opposite direction. The square red numbers on the digital clock beside his bed were a cruel reminder of the time – it would take him at least 10 minutes even if he ran the shortcut route to school, so he was definitely going to be late for the morning game day shoot-around.

Not a fun way to begin a Saturday.

Instead of cartoons, cereal and smiles around a family breakfast table, Matthew had awakened again to an empty apartment. No telling where dad had spent the night, and the night would likely bring another bad ending on the court as well, since they were set to play Thompson High that evening.

Matthew arrived at the gym and was seven minutes late.

He had barely made it to the school grounds when Mark's body sprang from the door of his grandmother's parked Camry. Mark was holding his cell phone and flailing his arms, excited by the text message on the display screen that he waved as he ran. Mark nearly tackled Matthew before he reached the walkway to the gym, and repeated with passion the news that there would be no team activities today.

"No practice, Man! No Practice... Maybe no game either!"

Matthew processed the information and waited for the details that Mark could provide.

"Coach Dudley left last night after the game–and told the principal he had a brother in Delaware that's dying. He could be gone for A WHILE, man! Can you believe it?" Mark's open left hand swung out and landed firmly on Matthew's back as a hearty exclamation point.

"Wow" is all Matthew could muster. That there was no shoot-around did seem a reprieve, of sorts, from the negativity they had been accustomed to over the last couple of weeks. But as fortunate as Mark had deemed it, Matthew quickly began to search his mind for something that would fill the time. If not this, what would he do all morning?

He didn't want to go back home and sit in a empty apartment all day. No computer, no phone, and precious little to choose from to eat other than peanut butter, some leftover pizza, saltine crackers and half a pitcher of grape Kool-Aid.

"I wanted to stay here to make sure you heard. Your phone musta not been working this morning. Anyway, I think most everybody else got the call from Principal Meeks, or saw the note on the window up there."

He pointed to the gym's front doors and continued to search Matthew's eyes for a hint of shared enthusiasm about the news.

"Wow." Matthew repeated. "So no game tonight, either, huh?"

"Prob'ly not – principal told Gramma that they'd prob'ly have to reschedule for later this year. Guess it depends on what happens with Dudley's Brother…"

Matthew nodded, and waved into the car at Mark's white-haired Gramma.

You could see the resemblance in her face – both she and her grandson had the same tiny round nose. And they also shared shallow happy eyes that seemed to anticipate finding a similar cheerful contentment in everyone around them.

"Well thanks for waiting here to tell me…" Matthew flashed a smile to affirm that all was well for both of them. "Looks like I get a few more hours sleep" he said, and waving to Mark, started to turn back toward the path he had just walked.

Mark called after him as he moved to re-enter the passenger side of the Camry. "See ya Monday, then! Tell yer dad I said hi!"

Matthew waved a goodbye over his shoulder as he walked away, and then snorted at the idea to himself.

His dad had always been entertaining, especially around any of his school friends. Life of the party.

But recently he just never seemed to leave the party to come home.

As soon as Matthew entered the shortcut path that led through the woods and toward the street where his apartments waited, three blocks away, he stopped and bent over to blow into his clenched hands, then rubbed them together for warmth.

He would wait here long enough to let Mark and his Gramma turn the corner, then head back to the Hebrews High gym.

CHAPTER 3

AN INTRODUCTION

IT WASN'T DIFFICULT CIRCLING BACK AND sneaking into the back door of the gym. A firm jiggle of the handle and strong yank upwards and out on the left side of the double doors and the latch gave way.

He would at least be able to get up a few hundred shots and stay busy.

The air in the gym was stale and smelled like a mixture of popcorn and sweat.

The lights had been left on from the night before – there would be no need to find the light key from Coach's office desk.

He walked downstairs and took off his jacket and sweat pants, leaving them on the floor of the gym, and grabbed two balls from the rack that had been rolled back into their locker room the night before. Two minutes later, he was going full speed up and down the floor dribbling both balls at the same time –

quick starts and stops, changing directions, eyes on the rim for court vision.

Matthew worked up a good sweat, and for the next 45 minutes alternated between these ball-handling drills, a couple of chair shooting drills, and free throws while he rested in between.

It kept his mind off his list of worries. That was one thing he thought he remembered from his mother – a busy body clears your mind.

"You're special – you know that?"

Matthew heard the voice from the free throw line as the ball swished through the net. He looked up and saw the same bearded man from the night before, this time sitting on the visitor's bench at the other end of the court.

"Matthew Patterson. Invited to join the Hebrews varsity team as a sophomore after just moving here last summer. You were brought here – hundreds of miles from where you grew up – because your dad wanted to run away from your mom's memory. With nobody right there all the time to tell you what to do, you've done pretty well.

But you and I both know you're capable of much more."

The man looked just as he had the night before – same jeans and tan shirt – but this time there was no broom. He rose up slowly from the bench to move in Matthew's direction.

Matthew wasn't sure what to do. The janitor guy couldn't know all of that about him.

He didn't even remember noticing the guy until last night... and now, thought Matthew, he somehow knows my life story?

"I'll rebound for you" the custodian said, and fetched the ball that had stopped bouncing near the baseline to return it to Matthew, kindly.

"How do you know all that?" Matthew's voice jabbed back at him, defensive and incredulous, as the ball met his hands. "Who ARE you?"

"People don't normally look for me until they need help with something, but I've been here for a good while now. And I'm hoping to help both you and your teammates."

Matthew waited for the answer to his first question.

The janitor rubbed his beard, then lowered his hand and shook the keychain that hung from a clasp on the side of his belt. "I have access to everything with these... and because people say and do things all the time without noticing I'm there, I hear things."

"So how are you gonna help us?" Matthew asked.

"I suppose it's up to the principal to make it official. But with Coach Dudley gone for a while, I offered to fill in and help carry you guys through a tough time. That's why I'm up here today – Meeks called me to meet in his office earlier."

Matthew nodded, and set his feet again, squaring his shoulders to the basket for another free throw as he spoke. "Well, good luck I guess."

The janitor smiled at him from the baseline, and quietly returned Matthew's next many foul shots to him after rebounding them. After finishing a set of twenty, Matthew said it was probably getting time for him to go, and walked over to pick up his sweat pants and jacket.

"You know, Matthew... whether I'm named coach or not, I know that someone has great plans for you. You have a future. And your teammates have no idea what you might help them become. But it all starts with this..." The custodian clenched his fist again and shook twice in front of his shoulder as he had the night before.

Matthew stared blankly, and waited. The custodian paused a moment, then tapped Matthew's chest and said: "It all starts with you."

"What do you mean? Why me?"

"You can't change others, Matthew – but I can help you with yourself. And you can inspire others to follow your lead if the change in you is positive enough to be visible! What I meant a moment ago is that, to get tougher, you need to stop dropping your chin, and start shaking your fist. Now – why don't you try it?"

Matthew had pulled his sweat pants on over his shorts, and held the jacket in his left hand while making a weak fist with his right hand. He barely moved it, eyebrows raised above a smirking frown of skepticism.

"Oh. No. That won't do... Everything starts with belief, kiddo."

The janitor looked up at the empty stands, to the ceiling lights, and then back at Matthew before he continued to talk.

"Have faith in what I'm saying, Matthew. My words are a gift that will guide you and bring you more than just success. Listening to me will bring you the significance."

Was this a janitor talking to him?

"You know," he continued. "Results aren't determined by what you are capable of doing – they're all about what you are willing to actually do... So make a fist, and that's what we'll use to make you a winner."

Matthew still hesitated, then slid his hand inside the jacket and pulled it on. This all seemed a little too bizarre to him. Before he could speak to excuse himself, though, the janitor waved off his obvious discomfort.

"You know – Matthew, that's okay for today. Your doubts are nothing I haven't seen before. How about I make a believer out of you anyway?"

He finished the last of that sentence with a comforting smile, and then turned to walk up the gym steps toward the administration hallway. "I'll see you Monday."

Instead of replacing them, as he always did, Matthew left the two balls he had been using on the gym floor and left quickly. The note that Matthew mentioned flew up when the door opened as the air hit it, and Matthew jogged the entire ten minutes back to his apartment.

His father was there, asleep in his bed, when Matthew arrived back home, and the rest of the weekend went by as an uneventful blur of TV and leftover pizza.

CHAPTER 4

MONDAY'S ANNOUNCEMENT

THE ENTIRE HEBREWS BOYS' BASKETBALL team was called to the office conference room at the beginning of first period. Some of them, like Mark, were still giddy without thought of what might be coming, just glad to be free of the tyrannical barking of Coach Dudley.

A couple, including Paul, sat detached and indifferent – apparently confident that no matter what announcement was made, they were going to remain bottom feeders this season. Where Mark was the puppy-dog optimist, Paul carried himself with a much more disinterested demeanor. Paul Sanders, a senior, was one of the strongest talents on the team – but his attitude was rotten.

The rest seemed curious, and at least somewhat pleased that the situation had drawn them out of their normal class schedules.

When the principal walked in, they drew their conversations to a close and adjusted themselves to sit upright and listen to his update on Coach Dudley.

Matthew hardly recognized the man that came in to stand behind the principal.

"Good morning, boys. As I shared with many of your parents on Saturday, Coach Dudley has had some unfortunate news and has had to withdraw from his position to attend to family matters for an undetermined length of time."

Principal Meeks scanned their faces and continued with a deeper, sterner tone. "Due to our school's size, and Coach Dudley's tradition of coaching without the help of any assistants, there was no obvious replacement on staff, although policy dictates that the position must be filled with someone under contract with us."

It was at that moment the principal turned his body and motioned with his open hand turned upward to introduce the janitor who had spoken to Matthew only two days ago.

The beard had been shaved clean, although the brown hair remained intact as Matthew remembered it. Instead of jeans and the tan shirt, he wore khakis slacks and a white button-down dress shirt with no tie. His smile warmed the room, and Mathew noticed him scan the room to share his quiet confidence and comforting glance with everyone.

The principal spoke again. "Our good fortune, though, has brought a very qualified interim instructor for your team who has been with us for some time. Mister Joshua Carpenter will be handling all coaching duties until Mr. Dudley returns. I trust that you will appreciate his offer to assist us, and I will let him say a few words now."

"Thank you, Mr. Meeks," he said, and the principal left them together in the room.

"Hello, team. It is my pleasure to have this chance to get closer to each of you. I am excited at what I hope to accomplish in the time we have together, and I am confident that this team can have a terrific season."

Tommy, sitting two chairs away from Matthew, mumbled quietly to himself, "I doubt it…"

Mr. Carpenter, the janitor (now coach), made quiet eye contact again with every player, and then sought to conclude what was a very short introduction speech.

"I know you have classes you need to get back to right now, but practice times from here on will be the same that you have listed on your calendars. Our next game is to-morrow, so I'll see you this afternoon to get started!"

Peter elbowed Paul, who sat beside him, and asked, "This guy's a janitor, man!"

His voice came out much louder than he intended, though, and it was clear that everyone had heard him when eyes all turned to him, then quickly back to their new coach for his response.

"Yes, Peter – I am a janitor here, a custodian of this campus… and now I'm your coach."

"So is he a janitor or custodian?" asked Paul under his breath, a wry smile spreading for his peers.

"Is there a difference?" Tommy whispered to Phillip, trying to straddle the line between respectful curiosity and still fit in with Paul's derision.

The new coach just continued to smile warmly, as he had when Matthew had grown uncomfortable the first time they had met.

"A janitor is kept around to clean up any messes and repair things, while a custodian is supposed to be someone who guards and maintains people or property. So I guess I would be both. But as a coach, I hope you will not take for granted what I can share with you."

"So what should we call you?" asked Paul.

"That's up to you. But be on time this afternoon, and come ready to work together. Now, you guys need to get back to your class." And with that, he turned and left the conference room, then walked out of the administration offices toward the gym.

It was during lunch that Matthew saw him next. Instead of eating in the cafeteria, he had made a habit of bringing the school Styrofoam tray into the gym – sometimes to study, sometimes just to be here where he felt more comfortable alone.

He found the custodian sitting in Coach Dudley's office, watching game film.

"So you were serious, huh?"

His new coach didn't immediately answer, but did pause the DVD player with Paul's body frozen a foot in the air, having just pulled down a rebound during the third quarter of Friday's game – the last one they had played.

"Mr. Carpenter – you really coached all-stars before?"

The janitor still hadn't looked up, but seemed to speak to the frozen screen of the TV instead. "That fist you need won't just happen without work – I'll need to help you learn to use of all your fingers first... Let's start with your number one finger, then."

"Coach – I can use my fingers just fine. I don't know what you..."

The janitor made a "number-one" sign, holding his pointer finger up in the air and waiting for Matthew's attention. "Going anywhere starts with your first finger..."

Matthew moved a bit in the doorway, positioning himself inside the office so he could better focus on what was being said. The new coach's voice was deep and confident and soaked through into the empty spaces deep within him.

"You've been treading water, Matthew. Think you're frustrated from giving all that effort on the basketball floor without any production? Imagine what it feels like for someone who has sleepwalked through a job they never really liked for 20 years without having any real impact or accomplishing what they might have.

Or think of a man who looks back after spending 20 years of his life distracted by video games or wasting his time on diversions and having nothing of significance to show for it. If you don't decide on where you want to row, you'll never get there!"

Matthew didn't quite get his meaning.

"Okay, son – I like to use metaphors. See, the place you want to row to, that's your destination – and that, together with a date you will get there, is your goal. If you have no goal, you've got no reason to row... so you end up just treading water. Make sense to you now?"

"Yes, sir."

"Good. Now that's where your finger comes in. Frustration is a symptom of higher aspirations – but like a runny nose, you will be miserable if you focus on the snozzle and feel sorry for yourself... you've got to take your medicine and soon you'll be better! Frustration is gift – it lets you know that you are wasting your time and need to change something. And all that anger and helplessness you are feeling is usually only the result of forgetting your first finger!

Now stay with me here – because this is important. Millions of people just tread water day after day and year after year because they never decide on the paradise they want to row toward. Too many of your friends think they have to wait for something to happen to them – they think that they are supposed to graduate from school and go find themselves. And the truth is, you can't find yourself. You create yourself. And you create yourself by choosing what island you will row to.

Matthew – if you don't choose an island, you'll either drift around and land somewhere by chance, or you'll wear yourself out with regret for never rowing your boat to it. But the great thing I want you to know is that whether you are 9 or 99, if you've been treading water for years or if you've chosen to row to the wrong island before, your journey doesn't HAVE to end there! You can always choose a new island – and that is what makes life interesting!"

Matthew still stood just inside the office doorway, but was listening attentively and found himself caring about what the man said. "I think I get it. But what does rowing have to do with our basketball team?"

The new coach sighed and then smiled back.

"What is the one thing you want to be or do more than anything right now?"

"I want a win!"

"Just one win – is that goal worth all the effort and sweat you've given?"

Matthew frowned, and thought a moment before answering. "No, sir. You know, I want us to go to the state playoffs. Coach Dudley says our school hasn't done that in over 20 years. He said all preseason that this group of players could take our school to the Promised Land."

"Okay – then let's get you there. That is your number one thing. That is your pointer finger, and the first piece of your fist!"

"That's where I want to row to, right?"

"You got it, Matthew. But it isn't that easy for everyone. Some people spend their whole lives without identifying what it is that they really want for themselves. Tell me – have you ever looked into a puddle when it has just been hit by a raindrop or two?"

"I don't think so…"

"Well, finding your one thing – your heart's destination – can be like looking into a rough patch of water. Sometimes you need to give it time to come into focus. It may not be clear at first, but if you are patient and keep looking until the ripples grow calm, eventually you will see it. Now, once you've determined what your one thing is and when you plan to achieve it, you have to write it down. You have to keep it in front of you and SEE it all the time. If it is truly important to you, you'll focus on that one thing all day long."

"Coach Dudley was always telling us we needed to focus more."

"He was right about focus, but may not have been very clear about what he meant when he said that to you."

Matthew nodded. There were lots of things Coach Dudley had said, often loudly, but seldom went into any detail about or explained so they understood why it was important or how to do it.

"See, you've got one pointer finger" the janitor continued, "only one. That is the definition of focus. Farmers used to say that 'if you chase two rabbits you won't catch either of them.' Same way with rowing – you have to choose your island and row like crazy to get there. And if there is anything in your life that would keep you from getting there, it must be removed from the picture you are painting. If there is a bad habit or unnecessary activity that will keep you from getting where you need to go, you need to cut it out of your life."

"Yes, sir. I understand. Our team needs to agree on an island. You know, Coach Dudley put up a poster up in the locker room about us making state, but some of the guys on the team just roll their eyes at it."

"You know, Matthew – I bet they are the same ones who think the team's offenses are flawed – the same ones who complain that he yells too much, or find a way to point blame him when anything else breaks down. Am I right?"

"Yes, sir. Especially Paul. He acts like Coach is an idiot. And I think after these last few losses, he's swaying some others to believe it, too."

The lights from the locker room seemed brighter, and shown through the office window casting a fluorescent glow on both of them throughout the entire conversation. It was the clearest that Matthew had thought in years, the most excited he had been, and he knew in his gut that this was the one of the most important talks of his life so far.

"Here's what you need to do, Matthew. Stop dwelling on your doubt. Know that making excuses never improved any situation. The stuff that has kept your team from winning so far has nothing to do with what your coach was asking you to do. Even when management does make it difficult – even if your coach did have you running a crazy offense – making excuses is never productive. If you blame others for where you are, you give away the ability to change where you are. Successful people find a way to overcome the obstacles they encounter – and if you are truly going to be a leader, you will get your team to stop focusing on what they cannot control, and start focusing on where they want to be and what you can control to get each other there!"

Matthew heard the bell chiming throughout the campus to signal the end of the period. His uneaten chicken nuggets had grown cold beside the fries and boiled stack of broccoli on his plate, but he wasn't thinking about being hungry.

"Thanks Coach Carpenter... I appreciate the talk."

"No more doubt. The number one finger reminds you to choose your island. Write it down... put it on paper so you can SEE IT. Make that island the one thing you focus on. And I'll see you later today at practice, right?"

"Yes, sir"

His team had already lost five games this season. As frustrated as he had been a few days ago, he was now focused on and excited about working to make the state playoffs.

Matthew backed out of the office, and wound his way down the hallway, through the gym, and back to the math hall for his next class, looking forward to what he expected would be a very different experience that afternoon.

He had a hope, and a future, and a voice to guide him – and about three hours until practice.

CHAPTER 5

TEAM INTRODUCTIONS

THERE WAS NO SIGN OF COACH CARPENTER in the gym after school when the guys arrived on their way to the locker room to change for practice.

They got their practice jerseys and shorts on. Bart, a modestly talented junior just glad to be part of the program, grabbed the rack of balls, and they eventually all made their way onto the court.

Some started taking long shots for fun, some stood around waiting and talking with one another, and a few worked on free throws or dribbling by themselves. Matthew was at a free throw line when their new coach made his entrance.

The coach walked quietly to the center of the court and waited for all movements to cease, for the balls to be held or stop bouncing, and all eyes to find him before speaking.

"Talent is important. You have to have talent to win..."

He looked around for a few moments as the players all began to slowly step in his direction to form a very imperfect circle.

"Talent is important," He repeated. "But this team has talent. If you were wondering why this group has underachieved so far this season – if you wondered why you've only won one of your first eight games – the first ten minutes of your practice time is all the answer anyone needs."

Nobody spoke or moved as he talked to them.

"The greatest moments of your life will be spent as a small part of something larger and more significant than yourself alone. And from what I've seen, our problem right now isn't skill or size. We need to get on the same page and learn how to play together, and stay disciplined and motivated in the midst of a little adversity."

It wasn't fear that held their attention, but a curiosity about his intentions and surprise with his honest acknowledgement of what each of them knew was true.

"So, what do we do today. First, I make sure you understand that from now on, when you are here together, everything we do is organized, competitive, and with a purpose. We don't have five different groups doing their own thing at half speed. We show up to get better, to grow closer, and we don't let our teammates forget why you're here. Got it?"

There were mumblings, scattered agreement, but no strong response by anyone.

"GOT it?" he repeated, with more volume.

"Yes, sir," came the intended reply, from all twelve –
some more enthusiastic than others.

"Alright. Does everyone here know our half-court
offense vs. both man and zone?"

"Yes, sir."

"Does everyone here know the secondary break
options?"

"Yes, sir."

"Does everyone here know their responsibilities and
help rotations in our man to man and press defense?"

"Yes, sir," they said again.

"Does everyone here know all of our inbounds
plays for side, corner, and baseline?"

"Yes, sir," they said, clearly becoming rote and tired
of the repetition.

"Good. Then let's go spend some time in the
locker room!"

Coach Carpenter jogged off ahead of them, and the
players all stood there and shared confused and uneasy
glances. Matthew wasn't the first to start toward the
locker room behind him – that was Simon – but he
smiled knowingly to himself as he jogged in beside the
others and heard their rumblings. This was definitely
something different.

When they got into the locker room, he directed
them to sit in a circle on the floor, and said he wanted
to start by asking them one question. "Don't answer
out loud! I want you to think about it, and we can discuss it later this week. But the question I want you to
answer for yourself is, why you are here?"

He nodded ever so slightly at Matthew as his eyes scanned the group.

"You have all the resources and gear you need. And once you decide why you are here and what you want to accomplish, the next step is learning who you have on your team to help make that happen..."

The rest of the two hour practice session was not a normal basketball practice. It was just a lot of talking to each other. The coach had them tell about their parents, any brothers or sisters, where they were from, where they had been, where they planned to be in the future, what their favorite toy was when they were younger, and even their favorite movie.

There was no sweating, and no bickering, but Matthew was concerned that they weren't getting ready to play Union Grove. They hadn't gone over a scouting report, hadn't run through or practiced defending any plays, or gotten up hardly any shots at all since last Friday, except for the casual stuff that coach had been upset about.

When the custodian was ready to end their practice time together, he asked them to move closer and make a tight circle. "Okay, guys. I know we've not spent any time on the floor working on skills, but this was more important today. Everything is built on relationships, and you have to know your teammate to care about and play hard for him. We can go over a walkthrough of Union Grove's plays and get some shots up tomorrow morning at shoot-around. Be here at 7:45 ready to go – and if one is working on free throws, we all are... got it?"

"Yes, sir" they answered, and split to change out of what were still pretty fresh uniforms that wouldn't need cleaning.

The new coach went into Coach Dudley's office, and the players grabbed their things and left the building to the sounds of the girls' team squeaking their feet on defense and balls bouncing as they competed in their practice drills.

Matthew was glad to see his dad when he got home, but they had only a brief and superficial conversation over microwaved chicken pot pies before Matthew went into his room and stared up at the ceiling, thinking of what he could do to help get his team to commit to reaching the same destination he desired.

CHAPTER 6

MORNING SHOOTAROUND

THE NEXT DAY MATTHEW WAS OUTSIDE the gym when Coach Carpenter arrived at 7:05am.

"Morning, Coach!" His eyes were bright, and his smile beamed enthusiasm.

The coach was surprised and pleased to have Matthew in such a good mood. Maybe his positive energy would be good for the team as they prepared for the Union Grove game tonight.

As coach held the gym door open, Matthew entered.

"Hey, I've been thinking a lot about what you said the other day. Can I talk to the guys for a few minutes before morning walkthrough? I want to make sure we're all on the same page, you know?"

"Sure, Matthew. You can take the first fifteen minutes. That good enough?"

"Yes sir!"

The next half hour leading up to their 7:45am game-day walkthrough seemed to last forever as Matthew work on two-ball dribbling drills and form shooting – all the while running over in his mind what he would say to his teammates. The janitor had inspired him. They needed to commit to rowing to the same island – and everyone had to see it as clearly as he did!

When his other teammates had all arrived, coach interrupted their individual free throw shooting with an announcement.

"All right, fellas – Matthew got here early and asked to have a players-only meeting... so everybody into the locker room. Matthew, they're yours for the next fifteen minutes."

Matthew watched as they moved off the floor. Some of them, like James, walked alone. James was a left handed shooter, but had started to lose confidence in his shot and had pulled away the last few days into the silent shell of his own thoughts.

Others, like Mark and Simon, walked in pairs talking amongst themselves. One pair walked more slowly, almost already convinced of the uselessness of this or any other team activity. Paul and Tommy had resigned themselves to just going through the motions. The janitor was right – after only seven losses, they were clearly only planning to tread water the rest of the season.

He followed Paul and Tommy, the last pair to get there, into the locker room and closed the door.

He waited for a few moments to let everyone sit and adjust themselves.

"Okay Matthew – what's up?" Luke asked. Luke was a red headed gangly kid who moved faster than you thought he could. He was their best on-ball defender and played with the focus and intensity of a man who refused to let anyone get the best of him.

Paul jabbed at him next. "Yeah – hurry up. I wanna spend some time with the ladies before homeroom!" Paul's eyes searched the other players around him for hints of agreement with his implied sense of being somehow inconvenienced.

Matthew just stood there, quiet. It was nearly a full minute of silence later that he began to talk. "I guess we only have about twelve minutes left, so I'd better talk fast."

He looked around and made sure to establish eye contact with each of his eleven teammates. "So, why are you guys here?"

He let it hang there for a moment – not expecting (and not getting) any response but bemused silence from some of them.

"Well, I'll tell you what I think. I think most of you are here for the same reason I am – you want to win and you think we have a group of guys here that can make this season something special...

But for some of you, maybe it's not the same. Maybe you felt pushed to be here by your parents, or maybe you are here because you think it is how you are getting into college, or maybe you were excited about the season but now you've started to doubt what we can be and just want to go through the motions for the next eight weeks..."

He paused and looked around at each of them again.

"But I am here to WIN! And winners don't drop their heads and give up because they failed a few times. Winners keep working until they get what they want. Because when you DECIDE to go somewhere, you will find a way to make it happen. You just have to know where you want to go."

Paul sighed heavily enough for everyone to hear it, and rolled his eyes.

"See that?" Matthew pointed to Paul. "That's what some of you are doing inside. You sigh and act too cool to commit to doing anything that might make you look bad. Remember the sign over there?" He pointed to the wall where Coach Dudley had placed the goals for this year's team. State Playoffs was in huge letters at the bottom of the poster.

"THAT is why I'M here! And I didn't know until last night how important that sign was! But last week, I sat here all upset – like some of you are now – and frustrated, and I felt like there was nothing I could do to make it better. I felt like I had done all this work, run all these sprints, put up who knows how many shots – and it was all just wasted effort."

Most of the team was listening to him now, nodding.

"So last night, when I got home, I kept thinking that we gotta stop treading water and start rowing to our island. And what I mean is that everything we do has to be based on getting where we want to be. And that's our island!" He pointed again to the poster.

"Luke – the state playoffs are being held downtown at Tech. How'd you like to walk out onto that floor to play? Paul, do you know how loud that gym gets when it's full? Can you imagine hearing them when you knock down a three to give us the lead?

Tommy, can you see yourself there at the free throw line, with ten thousand eyes watching as you ice the game at the end? Mark, can you feel us all huddled together and screaming and jumping after the buzzer? Can you guys imagine wearing our state tournament t-shirts to school the next Monday? That is where we want to go, guys!"

He could sense there was a rising belief in the room, an excitement that had slowly dissipated over the last seven games. He wanted to build on that.

"School is important – and we all need to keep our grades up. But the ONE THING I want out of this year is that memory. I want to be covered in sweat and standing on Tech's floor with a smile watching the rest of you guys do the same thing. And that has to be your ONE THING."

He held up his pointer finger. "That has to be the most important thing in our life right now. You've got to think about it every morning when you wake up – put a picture of it on your bathroom mirror. You've got to close your eyes and SEE it before you go to sleep at night and imagine how great it's going to be when we make it happen. We've got to decide that instead of just showing up to practice, we are showing up with a purpose. We are showing up to get our team to play on Tech's floor."

His right pointer finger was still in the air as he reached into his pocket with his other hand and pulled out a red sharpie.

"If you can SEE us at Tech – if you are willing to work like crazy so that every drill we do gets us one step closer to being there, then I think you should sign that poster. If you really want to do something special – if you're not just here to waste time – then sign your name as a promise to the rest of us that your ONE THING is getting to the State Playoffs.

Coach Carpenter believes in us. He and Coach Dudley both have told us all that we can make it to the Promised Land... and for us today, that is Tech's gym. If you can SEE it, if you will focus on it every day and get rid of anything that is an obstacle, I know we can turn this season around and get there. Are you with me?"

He was relieved and overjoyed to see most of them jump up with clapping and yells of "Yeah!" and "Let's go!" Every teammate signed the poster. Even Paul and Tommy. And the team had a great walkthrough in preparation for that night's game at Percy.

After the walkthrough, the janitor asked him about the player meeting he had requested.

"So, what did you say to the guys in the locker room before starting today?"

"Go look at the poster in there, coach. I just asked them where we were going. I told them what I saw, and some of them didn't see it – but the more I described it, the more heads started to nod and I saw smiles for the first time in weeks!"

"I'm sure it was helpful, kiddo"

Matthew hoped it was.

CHAPTER 7

THE POWER OF WORDS

MATTHEW SAT ALONE ON THE BUS BACK TO Hebrews High, staring out the rectangular window into darkness.

They had arrived and played the first quarter with enthusiasm.

They really seemed closer and more focused. But then, when things got tighter and they lost the lead just before halftime, they did not respond well.

The final score was really uglier than the game had been. As soon as they got down by ten points, halfway through the third quarter, all air completely went out of their balloon. The fist that Matthew had been shaking forcefully to inspire his teammates during halftime to rally them eventually slowed, and had later released itself into an open palm that his forehead rested in – chin down again and heart heavy – following the final buzzer when he reached the visitor's locker room.

It was their fifth loss in a row.

He was embarrassed to have been so loud and optimistic that morning. He felt so ridiculously foolish now. And he beat himself up with internal rebukes the entire ride back to Hebrews High.

He was the last player to get off the bus, and he waited in the parking lot until everyone else had gone, then started his lonely walk home without going back into the gym at all.

The custodian he had listened to, the one he had expected to be there for him, had seemingly vanished immediately after the bus got back and was nowhere to be seen. Just one more guy who let him down. Matthew wondered if his dad would be home to ask about the game. That was exactly what he needed...

The sidewalk ended at the first stop sign beyond the school, and he remembered to step carefully as he made his way in the dark through the damp craggy path, littered by rocks and sinkholes.

The air was cold, and blew through the thin gold hooded sweatshirt that he wore over his uniform. Matthew thought to himself how silly he must have looked standing there in the locker room full of so much passion earlier that morning.

He was an idiot to think that a few words could change their season.

"Everything begins with words, Matthew!"

Matthew stopped immediately and turned around to see a white truck at the stop sign, where he thought the voice had come from. He couldn't quite identify the person in the driver's seat at first, but as his eyes adjusted to the lower level of light, he saw the custodian's smile, and eyes, and then recognized the brown head of hair sitting at the intersection, shielded partially from view by the stop sign itself.

He had on the same purple sweater that he had worn at the game, and his face contained the same calm confident warmth Matthew remembered.

"Thought you had disappeared on us."

"I was right there, nearby. Waited for everyone to get picked up. In fact, I was only coming this way to tell you I was especially proud of your speech this morning."

Matthew had moved quickly from being upset, to being startled, to now being angry.

"My speech? It was really your speech that I just wanted them to hear, too. And it was a complete waste of time! You tell me I need to SEE where we want to go – stop treading water and decide on a destination... but what good did that do us tonight?"

The janitor sat there listening, empathic and patient, without a sound and allowed Matthew to continue.

"I mean, now I look like a complete idiot. They'll never listen to me again!"

There was a pause as Matthew ran out of anger and waited for a response.

"Words are powerful, Matthew," the janitor said. "Once you decide what your one thing is, Matthew, it is your words that will breathe life into the destination you envision. You started that this morning. You got them to sign the poster. They began to really SEE the place and experience you were describing."

"Well, a lot of good it did to us. We had a good first quarter, but then most of the team gave in to Paul and Tommy's doubts as soon as a couple of bad things happened. Just one or two mistakes, and they stopped believing in our goal. This 'see it' motivational stuff is a waste of time."

The janitor continued their conversation there at the stop sign, and no other cars had arrived to interrupt. "Matthew, did you take a shower today?"

"Yeah. I'm going home to take another one in a few minutes to try and wash this smell of losing off of me."

The janitor chuckled. "Will you take a bath tomorrow, too?"

"Yes! Coach, are you crazy?" Matthew shook his head and started to walk away toward his apartments.

"Wait, Matthew. Don't you see? Motivation – visualizing your goal – they are both like taking a shower. The energy they give you don't last forever – it isn't meant to. It just gets you ready for the immediate challenges and obstacles you will face that day."

Matthew slowed, but didn't yet turn his head back.

"And – just like you learned today – a bath will last longer if you don't go rolling around in the mud! ... that's what your guys did, you know – you rolled around in dirty doubts!

The janitor spoke more loudly to ensure Matthew heard him from further away.

"After you SEE where you want to go, your words are what light the path to get there. There are always winds that could blow you off course, Matthew. And most of those winds are the negative words that other people speak. You can either believe the doubts of others and get blown off course, or you can choose to believe that what you started rowing toward is still there waiting... if you just stay motivated and keep rowing."

Matthew turned and the janitor was standing up just outside his driver's door. "Come on – let me give you a lift up the hill. It's cold."

"You know – even if I believed you, what good is my word now? We just got hammered tonight. Remember the team going in the tank the entire fourth quarter?"

"You getting in or walking?"

"Yeah, okay." And Matthew walked over to the passenger door and climber inside.

The seat was warm on his legs even through his warm-up suit, and he was glad to not have to dodge any half-frozen sinkholes in the dark on the path he normally used.

After closing the door, he turned to the coach, who had waited to continue his thought. "Matthew, look at me. Hear this clearly: Words create your reality."

Coach Carpenter let that linger in the air a few seconds. He began to pull away from the intersection and up the hill in the direction of Matthew's apartment complex.

"What you hear – whether it is you assaying it or someone else – that becomes true in your mind. If a young girl is told that she is worthless or dumb, that is the reality she grows up with – and those words often become a prison she may never break free of, if she doesn't replace them.

But the beautiful thing about the power of words is that you get to choose the ones you believe. Think about the people around you that are always positive and encouraging, and then think of those who are often negative and filling your ears with doubts or fears.

Steer clear of the negative voices. And Matthew, be aware that some of the most damaging conversations you have are with yourself!"

Matthew digested what he was hearing. He had been criticizing himself all night. Nobody else had said anything bad to him – he had inflicted all this damage to his confidence completely on his own.

"Think about your mind as a fertile field. Every day, you plant seeds on that field – and those seeds are thoughts and those thoughts are the words and ideas that you choose to accept from yourself and others. Your life will be the harvest of the seeds you allow to grow there, Matthew.

If you plant only bad seeds, or if you allow other people's negative words to settle there, you will not reap a great harvest. But if you weed out and refuse to plant the negative thoughts – if you fill your field with positive and motivating words, then your life will soon see those fruits ripening for you to enjoy. But the law of the harvest always applies – and the harvest isn't immediate. It requires work and patience. The discipline of planting and cultivating positive seeds, and weeding out the bad ones, is difficult."

He paused as they turned into the apartment entrance. "I guess no discipline seems pleasant or easy at the time – but later, it produces. So which building is yours?"

Matthew pointed to the left, and remembered the things he had said to himself during the game–remembered the things his teammates had said when things were not going their way. The janitor was right. His team had faltered because of the words they had chosen to believe. "So what do we do next, then," Matthew asked.

"Show me your thumb." The janitor's warm tone remained steady, and he didn't seem at all bothered or concerned by the rough location of Matthew's living situation.

Matthew made a "thumbs up" sign.

"That's what you do. Remember the fist we talked about? The first part was your pointer finger – it reminds you to SEE what you want or where you are going. Your thumb is the second part we'll discuss. It is the part of your fist that holds the others together, and when you hold it up like that it points back at you to remind you that the seed you allow in your field – the words you accept as true – are significant. They create your reality."

Matthew was staring down at his thumb. And as much as he wanted to believe, he still couldn't get rid of the sound of ridiculing comment he imagined coming from his teammates. "But what does holding up my thumb do to help my team trust me, huh?"

"You teach yourself first. Get better at replacing negative thoughts like 'we're just wasting our time!' with something positive you can repeat in tough times. Others can pick it up later, and draw confidence from your results. For some teams, a phrase might be "all in to win." For others, it might be something like "'we can do it' or 'dig deeper.'" Your pointer is to SEE IT, and your thumb is to SAY IT."

Matthew put his pointer and thumb together with the other three fingers fanned out, and then, sarcastically to himself, mumbled: "Okay then! I'll say positive things. But I don't think that is going to solve our problems."

The janitor nodded as he parked in front of the building Matthew had pointed at.

"You are right, Matthew. It will take time. But your team does trust you. They respect your passion, and they want to believe in the goals you've described. Your challenge is to have them replace the doubts they hear from others with the confidence of their own positive expectations and the encouragements of their teammates."

The new coach raised his eyebrows to emphasize his next point.

"But be sure – SAY IT involves more than just repeating positive affirmations. It also includes asking yourself the right questions. Instead of 'Why do I have to be here?', or 'When will the coach do things differently?', you need to begin asking 'What can I do to make this program better?' And finally, it requires your willingness to have difficult conversations with teammates if they are not meeting expectations you all agree on. But if what you SEE is important enough, you'll be willing to SAY that, won't you?"

Matthew looked up at the moon and knew what the custodian meant. "Yes sir. I think I know just what you mean. And I will."

He nodded goodbye as the truck backed away, and then waved to the two neighbors when he suddenly realized he was alone. As Matthew made his way through the building 400 main entrance, though, he didn't feel alone anymore. He could hear the words of his new coach still echoing in his mind.

He was already looking forward to their next practice.

CHAPTER 8

THE CHALLENGE

WITH WEDNESDAY CAME THUNDERSTORMS, and the dark rumbling grayness of the sky outside matched to mood that most of the players carried through the hallways between classes. There seemed to be an unspoken agreement between players and the rest of the student body that precluded anyone from discussing the past seven games.

Nobody wanted to make them feel any worse than they already did about opening the season with a record that now stood at 4-6. As long as it wasn't spoken of, there seemed the weight of those losses seemed easier to carry. All but one of the players was thankful for the consideration of not acknowledging their situation. Matthew didn't like it one bit.

He wasn't ashamed of where they were. Disappointed, yes – but to stop talking about it seemed like an admission of failure. If you were excited about something, you talked about it! The janitor had said to him that everything began with words. His guess was that those same things, if not spoken of, would begin die.

So during the day he said what everybody else was thinking.

"We lost both Friday and last night." But his tone was not sad or beaten, it was hopeful – as if the losses were all just a preamble to the important stuff that waited in the future.

When practice came, everyone seemed flat. There was no bounce in their step. The team seemed reluctant to give themselves permission to hustle or talk like they had in the preseason practices. They moved like meek dogs waiting to be kicked again by a cruel owner – knowing the next whack was coming soon.

Matthew kept his enthusiasm, though. He encouraged his teammates through warm-ups and they all stayed together as instructed through the pre-practice free throws and dribbling drills coach had asked for, but it seemed to have very little effect.

Coach Carpenter let them get through the first ten minutes or so, then blew his whistle and motioned for everyone to join him at one end of the floor.

"Guess you saw the practice plan I posted. Got yourselves through the introductory stuff I had written down."

"Yes, sir." Paul said, loudly. He was the unquestioned king of going through things without any real intensity.

"Did you notice anything about the rest of what I have planned?"

There was no answer. Other than the pre-practice stuff he had listed in some detail, it looked a lot like one of Coach Dudley's old practice plans.

"That's right! It's just about identical to what you've been asked to do before I got here. Seemed to me that there wasn't much wrong with what you were doing. I think the problem is how hard you're choosing to do it. If you want to blame anyone for where you are in life, look in the mirror a while. Assigning blame doesn't change anything. Changing yourself is what changes things, guys."

Many of Matthew's teammates looked down in acceptance of this fact.

"Practice is going to be full speed. We're going to go hard, or you won't be on the floor with us. Loafers are why they made that track around the top of the gym. Now, if you want practices to be loud, if you want practices to be competitive, if you want practices to be fun, that is completely up to you. But whatever you get out of practice, it will be you that is totally responsible for it. GOT it?"

The team nodded, and for the most part seemed relieved to hear him say what he had.

"Now, Paul, you get around the top a couple of times at full speed and you can rejoin us as we go through our shell work. Let's go, guys!"

There was a new energy throughout the rest of their practice that day, and Matthew felt, when it was over, that they really had gotten better. They had talked more, and pushed each other, and it wasn't negative.

They were encouraging and calling each other out to take care of details and it felt good.

After practice was over, Coach Carpenter told them that Thursday's practice would be in the locker room again – no need to dress out tomorrow. Just bring a pen and both ears.

When Thursday afternoon rolled around, the locker room was loud and boisterous. Chairs were set up in a large circle, just like when they had talked about themselves the week before, and each player filled one well ahead of schedule.

The janitor walked in wearing his customary jeans and tan work shirt at exactly 3:45, their normal practice start time, and he carried with him a large handful of 5x7 note cards that were passed out – a dozen to every player.

"So where are we going?"

The entire group answered "State playoffs" with varying degrees of energy.

"Where?"

"STATE playoffs!" they repeated – this time with more fire.

"Right. You have had your gear all season. Now you have your goal. So what do you know about the people that will help to get you there?"

The players looked around at each other, memories faded from only a few days ago, but bits and pieces of sibling names and parent's occupations and favorite childhood stories still flashed, even if incomplete, into the minds of the layers as they surveyed each other and tried to recall what had been shared by whom.

"Coach, I can't remember everything about everybody!" said Paul.

"You can if it's important, Paul. If you knew that you would be given ten million dollars for remembering the color, license plate, and model number of a vehicle and reciting it to the owner at 8am on his birthday, would you find a way to get and remember that information?"

"Hey, man, I'd do all kinds of things for ten million!"

"So you are saying you could do that?"

"Yes, sir – no problem!"

"You all could?" He asked the group.

They nodded and agreed excitedly.

"Then getting to know your teammates should be easy. Ten million dollars is just money. It doesn't sweat for you, or smile, or cry, or care at all about what happens to you or it. But these guys here..." he pointed motioned with his hand around the room.

"These guys here want the same thing you do. They are willing to spend hours and hours with you, lifting weights and diving and sprinting and sweating just to help you get what you want, because they want the same thing."

"Okay, Coach Carpenter, we get it. We need to get to know our teammates better. Is that what the note cards are for?"

"The note cards come after your test. First, you get to study. When you know enough to build a good relationship, then you can move on to setting expectations."

"What do you mean?" Matthew asked, sincerely puzzled.

"I will give you 60 minutes to memorize everything about your teammates we discussed a few days ago, then I will ask each of you a question. We will run one mile for every missed answer, and then you will remember. Success is built with relationships. When you get that, we can deal with the note cards."

An hour and a half later, after three missed questions and three long miles, they met in the locker room again. It was almost time for practice to be over, and rides would be arriving at the parking lot soon.

"Great – so now you know your teammates a bit better. Next, I want you to raise your right hand if you want to win."

Every player's right hand went up.

"Okay, now raise your left hand if you want to play most of the game."

As expected, every left hand was raised.

"Now look around. Since there are more than five left hands raised, we could have a problem with expectations. So let me be clear – the best will play more than the rest as long as the best don't rest when they're playing. I want effort at all times – because talent without intensity and discipline will be sitting next to me during games."

"Your homework is to identify the roles you and your teammates will be responsible for. Everyone has to contribute something to our cause. I want you to write down what you expect from each other. It's very simple. You have twelve cards. Write a teammate's name on each, and underneath it write down two specific things they will have to do for us to reach our goal this year. On the back, write down one thing they must stop doing for us to get there. Do not discuss your answers."

He paused, scanning the room to confirm their attention.

"Roles are important. But it's also important to remember that being on this team is a privilege. You are all part of a very special journey together to what will be a rewarding destination. Return the cards to me tomorrow before homeroom – I'll be in the coach's office."

CHAPTER 9

SETTING EXPECTATIONS

FRIDAY MORNING'S WALKTHROUGH HAD been replaced by sharing their expectations of what each team member needed to do, or not to do, for the team to get better. Everyone was pretty close in what they thought each player should contribute. Peer-suggested roles included Tommy needing to rebound, Keith needing to shoot lay-ups only and defend the opponent's best ball-handler, and Luke being their best shooter and needing to get back on defense more quickly.

The discussion went well, and Matthew felt he and his teammates were prepared for a good showing that night against Union Grove.

It was another away game, but Union Grove was not a traditionally strong team, and looking around the bus it seemed that his teammates shared the confidence he felt, and had really seemed to benefit from thinking about what each of them needed to do for the team to succeed.

He had been speaking positives to himself over the last three days, and his encouraging comments had begun to spread to others in Wednesday afternoon's practice. There were a number of players who applauded other's efforts with "Nice pass" and "Hands up closeout – good job!"

Matthew was pleased with how quickly the custodian's lessons had taken hold and created positive results. That morning, he woke up and didn't even mind seeing his dad lying passed out on the couch with the same clothes on from Thursday. Matthew simply thought to himself – SEE where you're going, and SAY positive things to build belief in your ability to get there. He made a pistol with his right hand and shook it as he got on the bus to ride over to Union Grove for their game.

And it was because of his optimism and confidence in the game's outcome that when halftime arrived with Hebrews down by nine points, Matthew was ready to explode. But Coach Carpenter beat him to it, storming into the visitor's locker room to share his concerns first

"Is that what you promised your teammates they could expect from you? Is that an effort you're proud of?" His voice was emotional, but controlled and firm.

"That half is over, got it? Now, you can pout about what's already happened or get focused on the future. We've got a long season still ahead of us, and I expect to get us to the state playoffs. But it looks to me like there's only one guy out here who believes we can do that!" He pointed at Matthew, and then shot a disappointed stare at Tommy, who had been sitting on the bench most of the second quarter after missing three block-outs on defense.

"Didn't each of you agree to do what your teammates talked about? Didn't each of you agree to work together and do your assigned jobs to get to state?" He looked around, and everyone on the team was listening. "Well, tell me – was your commitment to only work hard and believe in yourselves until the road got tough, Tommy, did you promise your teammates to rebound only when it was easy?"

His voice was clear and calm, but energized. "Now we have sixteen minutes left to make this right. When you come out of this room, it better be with intensity!"

He paused and considered his next words more carefully, then decided to leave it to them. "Decide what need to say to each other, and say it. This is your team, guys."

When the players were left alone in the locker room, there was a short wait before someone chose to speak. The first voice to rise above the mumbling was Paul's.

"Alright guys – pick it up – I want to get through this game without having to run too much at practice tomorrow."

Tommy, standing beside him, agreed. "Yeah – talk it up a little. Make it look good. Don't give coach a reason to turn this into track practice."

They started to walk out – but there was no purpose other than dodging punishment. Matthew was incredulous and heard himself yell "Stop!"

It hadn't even been something he planned to do, but here he was – again – in front of his team's increasingly frustrated and doubtful eyes.

"Don't give up and leave yet. That's not why we're here."

Tommy turned his head back with his hand still on the locker room door, held partially open.

"Listen, Patterson." He sighed, exasperated. "We don't want another pep talk. We need a coach, and we need better players. But right now we just need to get through this game. C'mon, guys."

"NO."

There was dead silence and nobody moved. This was the first real conflict that had occurred between teammates all year.

"What?" Tommy was shocked. As a senior, he had lived through losing seasons before. He had gotten used to the expectation of defeat, and here was a sophomore stepping out to challenge him?

"I said No. That's not why we're here, Tommy."

Matthew felt himself breathe in and then exhale deeply. This was the moment the custodian had talked about, saying something uncomfortable, and he felt the words just come as he stood there. They were his words, and his voice was clear as he spoke them.

"We're here to do something special. I didn't sign up to just 'get through' anything. And I don't think you did either. Just getting through isn't why I woke up this morning. It isn't why I did all the summer conditioning workouts. We're here to push each other and do whatever it takes – to get to where we said we would!"

Matthew's finger was pointing into the air, in the imagined direction of Tech's campus, and the Promised Land they had discussed.

"Our problem isn't our coach, or our offense, our uniforms, or the gym, or anything else. Our problem is that we said we wanted to go somewhere together, and then when things didn't come easily we started to believe in our doubts more than our destination!"

He jabbed his thumb into his own chest as he emphasized the next sentence.

"I get frustrated, too. But I still believe in what coach has told us – and what we promised each other with those signatures. I'm gonna go out there and play hard – not to get through tonight, but to work for the tomorrow I know we can have if we decide to work for it. But I can't do it by myself... you can't do anything great without a team around you. I need you guys. I want to stand together two months from now on Tech's floor and look back at today as the day we decided we weren't just interested in playing basketball – it'll be the day we decided we were committed to making the state playoffs."

He stood there waiting for their response – his chest heaving inside the purple #22 jersey.

The first hands to begin clapping were John's, but he was immediately joined by three or four others, and then the locker room was filled with shouts and claps and high fives and everyone converged on him to hold their hands high in the air. Even Tommy had moved into the cluster of bodies, smiling.

"All right!" he said, his voice gaining passion. "Then let's do it! Everyone here to make state, let's break on three and go have a good second half!"

Tommy was buying in. He winked at Matthew and yelled out – "One, two, three!"

"Knights!" they yelled together... and bodies rushed out the door back toward the gym.

Matthew trailed behind them in awe of what had just happened. He thought of the custodian's words and smiled, then made a fist – and shook it in front of him as he headed out to join his teammates on the floor.

"Okay, let's go!" he said to himself, and jogged to join his team.

CHAPTER 10

THE PROBLEM WITH OKAY

THEY LOST BY TWO.

The third quarter had begun with the intensity their new coach had requested, and by the end of the quarter they had actually taken a small lead. But in the fourth, with the score tied and play getting more and more physical, Tommy got hit with a firm forearm in his chest, and retaliated with a two handed shove and an explosion of profanity that the referees saw and heard, and quickly addressed.

The technical was Tommy's fifth foul, so he had to leave the game. Paul was angry at that, and Matthew got frustrated with Paul, and before long their team's confident poise and discipline had been sabotaged and Union Grove made their free throws down the stretch and Hebrews had lost.

With no game Saturday night, Coach Carpenter said that the gym would be open Saturday morning at

10:00am for shooting and skill work for those who wanted to come. Their next official practice would be Monday, after the girls finished.

The bus was almost completely silent, and Matthew jumped out and walked home briskly from the gym parking lot when they arrived, intent on not having any conversation with the janitor this time.

The next morning, though, with his head a bit more clear, he decided that if he was going to get better, if he was going to be a dependable leader, he had to show up. Being there was the least he should do if he wanted to improve his skills and friendships.

He pulled open the unlocked gym doors at 10:00am and was the only one there. After twenty minutes of two-ball dribbling and form shooting drills, he was still alone. He walked back to see if anyone was in the locker room. The janitor was busy moving their wet uniforms from the washer to the dryer.

Matthew walked in and sat down on a chair in the corner, waiting for his new coach to comment about Matthew being the only one who had shown.

"You know, you guys are right on schedule!"

Matthew turned his head slightly to one side, looking with disbelief at the man who was now closing the dryer with a smile.

"Failure is a great teacher, Matthew – where there is no failure, there's no reason for you to improve! Truth is, you've got them right where you want them to be – ready to listen!"

Matthew felt like they had already had this conversation before.

"Right" Matthew said, his tone rising and falling slowly to emphasize the sarcasm.

The janitor didn't respond, but waited for him to continue.

"Coach – they've already listened... and now they're shutting down again. This FIST stuff isn't making anything better. I thought we were going to be okay, but right now I just want to take this SEE finger and this SAY finger (he held up his right hand in the shape of a pistol) and shoot myself with them!"

The janitor smiled warmly. "Patience, Matthew. You are just being deceived by your doubts. If you truly want to enter the Promised Land your team has imagined, you will need to believe through the storms of adversity. Do not be afraid; keep on speaking, do not be silent."

The janitor reached out to hold Matthew's hand, then simply adjusted his fingers into a different shape, with his pointer finger and thumb making a circle.

"That is what you are right now. Exactly what you are – your team, that is... You are absolutely and completely okay... average, mediocre, and miserable! Isn't it great!

"What?" Matthew squinted his eyes and jutted out his jaw in confusion.

"Okay is not where you want to be, is it? That the team is miserable – most of them, at least... it means they want more – they're discontent – they have higher expectations than just being OKAY!"

Matthew was upset – "Now wait – I've thought about and put up pictures of where we are going. I made sure my teammates could all SEE what we are working for. Not only that, but I have been replacing my doubts and negative thoughts with the affirmations you said I should write out – I SAY them to myself and then I also SAY stuff to encourage my team, but it's not working! Why just me? If this stuff is important, why don't you say it to all of us at the same time in a team meeting or at practice?"

The janitor sighed before responding.

"Matthew, I've learned that changing the world, or even your corner of it, can only occur by changing one person at a time. The tiny ripple that their change creates can then become a tidal wave of influence. But not everyone is ready to hear what I have to say. Sometimes, their ego, or emotion, or false assumptions keep them from listening. All we can do is love them where they are, and share our guidance with those whose ears are open. Don't waste time screaming at those who choose to be deaf. Someday their circumstances will change, and they will open their ears as well. Do you understand?"

"I guess so…"

"Okay – so you SEE it, you SAY it – and that's okay… but okay isn't enough – right?"

"Not for me"

"Good. That's because positive thinking and visualization by themselves aren't enough for results to occur – you need to take action, and let actions become habits, and those habits will inspire others and produce your results!"

The janitor leaned against the washing machine he had just emptied, and opened held his right hand up as he spoke, with only his thumb, pointer, and middle finger extended.

"You've got to start-something next, kiddo."

"What do you mean?"

"See the finger there that, if you lifted up by itself, makes others think you want to start–something?"

"That's cute – but I still don't get it."

"What I mean is, it's okay to see what you want," he tucked his middle finger back into the fist and made an 'OK' sign. "And it's okay to talk about it, but to get beyond okay you have to start-something!"

"What do you want me to start, coach?"

"Matthew, that's up to you. But to have more, you sometimes have to do more – or do things smarter. If you are already practicing as much and as efficiently as you can in afternoons, then start something else. I'll make sure that we work smarter with the practice time we have each afternoon… but if that time is being well-spent, and you need to be a better shooter, then start a morning shooting workout.

If you need to be a better ball-handler to reduce turnovers, come in for extra ball-handling drills twice a week! If you need to see what you're doing in games to correct mistakes – start a breakfast film session. If you need to build better relationships, start spending more time with people outside of the gym... but whatever it is, nothing changes until you start something!"

Matthew felt overwhelmed. Wasn't he already coming in on his own? Wasn't he the only one that showed up for open gym today? Wasn't he doing enough already?

The janitor continued with an example.

"If you wanted to be a doctor, you could write that goal out, define the specialty you wanted to focus on, post pictures of doctors in your house, speak only positives and encourage yourself silly – and if you never applied to college, or if you struggled and refused to start studying when you arrived, you'd never wear that white coat!"

Matthew agreed with what he was saying, and agreed with him that you had to work instead of just daydream... but was unsure of what he needed to start doing more of.

"You know, Matthew, that is often that hardest part of getting results – people will plan and organize and prepare for years, and do just anything except actually getting started with something necessary to move them toward what they want. Now I know you're a pretty good worker. And I'm glad you're here today. But you can't ever let other people's lack of commitment affect your work ethic or determination.

Remember – hard work brings profit, but mere talk leads to poverty. And if you do start doing something different, it will eventually inspire others to join you because they'll see the change in you and want it for themselves.

So – any thoughts?"

Matthew looked at the floor plank for a few seconds, then nodded his head. He jumped up from his chair to speak.

"I think I might have an idea for Monday. I'll see you at practice, coach."

After he left the laundry room, Matthew put up another 50 free throws before leaving, but the janitor kept himself out of the gym.

Still, Matthew always felt much better after spending the time with him.

CHAPTER 11
GETTING STARTED

MONDAY WAS WARMER, AND MOST OF THE snow that had fallen over the weekend had melted into slushy puddles that students dodged, or jumped over, as the last bell rang and everyone made their way through the parking lot to find their bus.

Some players would go home, and then return later for second practice slot, since they shared the gym with the girls' team, after getting a snack or having dinner. Matthew usually stayed and took care of his schoolwork or surfed the internet in the media center for a while, then hung out in the locker room or went into the gym and watched the girls after dressing out.

It was this two hour block of time that Matthew decided to start something.

On their late weeks, he would go watch game tape right after school. Skill work wasn't their main weakness, so instead of more individual dribbling and shooting, he could spend that time with a teammate. He could get closer and spend time with guys he was depending on, and they could together see some of the on-court decision making, both good and bad.

Before homeroom, he spoke to Peter about it, but Peter refused and said he had too much to do. Then, in between second and third period, he had asked their other point guard, Keith, to join him in the locker room. Matthew was a little surprised when he agreed, and was able to set up the TV cart and DVD player in the locker room during lunch.

When Keith arrived, the television hissed with black and white snow. Matthew had two of their current season game DVD's in his hands, and was about to slide one into the video player drawer.

"I got these from Coach Carpenter" Matthew said, and though Keith assumed he was talking about the DVD's, Matthew went over to his locker and grabbed a couple of blue PowerAdes and two bags of chips.

They watched the video, and talked, and laughed, and by the time the PowerAde bottles were empty, they had spent a good 45 minutes together.

Matthew knew they would be better players and better friends because of it, and after returning the video equipment to the coach's office, they got dressed out and worked on their biology study guide together.

When the girls finished, Coach Carpenter began with a talk about accountability at midcourt.

"Team's get better because they care about each other and where they want to go together. They make decisions both on and off the floor based upon the knowledge that what they do will affect the other people. When you choose to make a bad decision, it is just like saying that your individual momentary desire, or anger, is more important than all these other people that are depending on you."

He turned to focus his attention on Tommy. "Do you have something to share?"

"Sorry for the tech, guys. I know I shouldn't have done that – especially in a close game."

"Not in any game. Violence," coach continued, "is the last resort of a limited intellect. I expect you to be physical, I refuse to allow violent – Got it?"

"Yes, sir."

"And one more thing. How many of you said anything to Tommy about his behavior?"

Nobody spoke up.

"Guys, there are two reasons you don't hold other's accountable for their job. Either you don't care enough about what we're here to accomplish, or you don't care enough about the person to help them make better decisions.

Parents hold their children accountable and discipline them because they care. If you care, you call somebody out and remind them what their responsibilities are. We are a team that cares – about each other, and our goal, right?"

"Yes, sir!"

"And we WILL hold each other accountable, right?"

"Yes, sir."

"RIGHT???" he asked, more loudly.

"YES, SIR!" they yelled.

"Then let's have a good practice. Tommy, when we're done, you owe ten laps around the top before going home."

The practice went pretty smoothly, and most everyone contributed to the constant chatter and encouragement and intensity of the drills and scrimmaging. The one other moment that was uncomfortable came during one of those half-court scrimmage sets, when Coach Carpenter stopped them to voice his disappointment with Paul's effort.

"Accountability includes making adjustments, fellas. Paul, go to the gold team. Phillip, you're taking his spot. If you don't play hard, you don't play. Just because you should be a starter doesn't mean you have to be if you're not willing to work."

Instead of causing a big stir, though, that moment seemed to make everyone more comfortable. They knew he deserved it – he knew it – and if they were going to get where they said they wanted to go, Paul would have to play harder.

When practice was over, Matthew actually heard Phillip go over and talk to him – but not to disparage the coach. He was telling him to pick it up and play harder for us – for his teammates. That, Matthew thought, was really a cool thing to hear.

CHAPTER 12

CLIMBING THE HILL

THAT TUESDAY NIGHT THEY WON THEIR fourth game of the season and beat Roman Hills.

Wednesday morning every player was proud to walk into their first period class with a renewed spirit and sense of accomplishment. The Knights had played an inspired game the night before, and even though Roman Hills kept it close early, the intensity and effort that Matthew, Tommy and their teammates gave created easy baskets and an eventual fourteen point win.

Before the game they had decided to start breaking their huddles with "Make State!," and even Tommy had taken time during pre-game in their locker room to remind everyone about Tech's floor, about where they would be in only a few short weeks after region playoffs. He described the gold-clad crowd and the smell of the wood floor and even told them where he wanted to eat with them as a pre-game meal.

Luke told everyone to stay positive and play through mistakes. Matthew added that they needed to stay loud and encourage each other – especially when something went wrong. Paul was a bit distant, but held in any doubts he might have had.

At halftime, with a five-point lead, they again reminded each other of the need to stay positive through any mistakes. It was great when Matthew heard his team yelling encouragements from the sideline even after a missed shot. The positive shouts had really made them play harder for each other, with more confidence, and the locker room and stands after the final buzzer were loud, full of smiles and high fives.

Wednesday after school, since they had late practice again, Matthew invited Luke come in to watch film. Peter had refused again, saying he was busy, but it was nice to have somebody to watch a replay of the previous night's game with, and he and Luke still were able to catch a few things they needed to improve.

When everyone had arrived in the locker room, the coach peeked in for what they thought was a pre-practice talk.

"Enjoy your win," coach said – and handed out two boxes of ice cream sandwiches

"Thanks!" and "Thanks, coach!" came a chorus of appreciation, as twelve high school guys grabbed two sandwiches each and inhaled them.

"You need to celebrate along the way, not just at the end of the season. Never let an opportunity to congratulate yourself or those you care about for a job done well!"

Practice on both Wednesday and Thursday went well and was productive. The playful jabs and competition that had nearly disappeared during their losing streak had returned.

Press attack runs and timed shooting – normally mundane drills – were alive with chatter and feeling of camaraderie. They were feeling good now, and Friday's game at Walker was a chance to go undefeated for the week.

Coach Carpenter didn't appear totally glad to have his team's enthusiasm up, though, and even refused to joke around with the players during water breaks. He emphasized in Thursday's pre-practice meeting that everyone had to focus on their roles, on playing the next game instead of celebrating the previous one.

But you could tell that a weight had lifted off his shoulders also, and he tried to find opportunities to build his players up with praise.

Friday, after shoot-around, like the Wednesday and Thursday before it, found Matthew and his teammates still walking with an extra bounce in their steps through the hallways, looking forward to the game against Walker that night. Walker was the only team in their region with a worse win-loss record than Hebrews, and everyone was glowing with positive expectations.

Then Hebrews lost to the worst team in their region.

Matthew reminded himself and his teammates throughout the game of where they were going, told them to talk positively to themselves and not get down. But there were so many mistakes! Walker had come out pressuring them, and they weren't prepared.

A couple of missed shots and three straight careless turnovers to open the third quarter, and the game slipped away. Then bench was silent by the end of the third quarter, and they eventually lost by eight points. Afterwards, as he scanned his teammates, Matthew again saw the confident glow had been drained from their faces.

The back slaps and smiles were again replaced with silence and muttering.

The janitor's post-game comments were short: "Practice tomorrow morning at 8:00am. Be ready to work."

Matthew made an attempt to salvage the night by again reminding his teammates about their destination and the significance of the things they said to themselves.

"Hey, guys – we're okay. We've got to stay together, though. Stay positive. We stopped talking when we got down after halftime. Let's come back tomorrow morning and fix that."

Still, there was only silence and frowns.

The only voice that followed was Tommy's "See you in the morning, fellas"

Instead of hopeful, it seemed more a deep foreboding sigh than an attempt to revitalize the troops. Saturday morning's practice was not going to be fun.

Once again, on his lonely walk home, Matthew felt like he was a barely flickering candle in the suffocating darkness of his team's frustration.

CHAPTER 13

COMMUNICATING COMMITMENT

SATURDAY'S PRACTICE WAS FULL OF LOOSE ball drills, rebounding wars, and taking charges.

"Resilient teams find a way to win. They bounce back. Keep running!"

The team was finishing up their six-pack of runs, one for each missed free throw that they had promised to be held accountable for.

"Strong teams talk to each other and keep themselves focused on their destination instead of looking down at whatever much they might have stepped in."

The baseline was now just a row of heaving chests and heavy breathing, hands resting on knees following the series of full court sprints.

"Grab your stuff, fellas. We're done for the day. Just remember – we are right now sitting at 4-9, and travel to Greene County on Tuesday. This is well past the halfway point of your season. We've got some growing to do if we want to go into the region tournament with a legitimate chance to make a run into state."

Instead of everyone just walking back to the locker room, though, Matthew called them all into a tight huddle under the basket.

"One, two, three: Make State!" they yelled, and jogged back together.

"Matthew!"

Matthew stopped at the hallway doors.

"I need to see you in my office, kiddo."

And with that, the custodian led him to another meeting in the coach's office and closed the door. From where he sat, Matthew could see his teammates occasionally moving past the window while Coach Carpenter spoke.

"You plan on wearing a wedding ring someday, Matthew?"

"Do I what, sir?"

"You know. A wedding ring. Round gold thing to put on your finger. Do you plan to wear one when you get married?"

"I suppose, coach."

"Why is that?"

This was too weird. Matthew had no idea where he was going, but by this time had learned to trust and let the custodian lead him where he intended.

"Um… I guess so my wife won't get mad at me. So everybody knows I'm married."

"That's right, Matthew. You'll wear it to let others know that there is someone important to you that you have committed yourself to caring for. That's the next finger I want to talk about – it's time you learned to share more."

"Learn to what?" Matthew tried to mask his irritation, but couldn't.

"Your ring finger – you have to let others know you're committed to something special and share your enthusiasm, your vision, your words, your plan of action – it's not just about seeing it, saying it, and starting it – you have to share it with others."

"You mean part of the fist! Okay, I see. Next thing to get better is to share stuff?"

"Correct! Matthew, when you share your goals and dreams, two things happen. First, you begin to build support and gather enough talent and effort to make something happen that you could never accomplish by yourself, and second, you advertise that commitment by everyone to accomplishing the goal because you promise each other to row together!"

It made sense, he thought. After all the stuff he had been doing on his own, to be asked to tell others and get them more involved was actually a welcome request.

"Nothing great can be accomplished by yourself alone. Even in golf, there are caddies and swing coaches and spouses and sponsors. Nobody becomes a success by themselves, and the wisest among us learn that it takes a team to do anything truly worthwhile.

You need a team, but not a team of employees. Recruit owners, who are excited to share in the profits and the process, that are willing to invest themselves and do work to create something that they care about. You build that support first by announcing your destination, and finding others who want to take the same trip."

The custodian continued, pointing to a game schedule on the wall as he began again.

"That's why we publish a schedule with the state tournament dates included. It is why you wear our team t-shirts to school, and why break your huddles saying 'make state!' And you also share your goals with others so they can help you along the way. The universe moves when you announce your dreams, and you will be amazed what can happen when providence steps in to provide unexpected assistance to your cause."

He waited to allow that last part settle into Matthew's memory.

"You share and advertise and publish and broadcast your goal until you get there. And when you do that, you'll learn who is really interested in rowing with you, who is only interested in riding, and who is spiteful enough to poke holes in the boat."

"Poke holes?"

"Rowing metaphor again. Sorry. But you see, not everybody will want go to where you do – some just want to be out on the water… but it's your job to make sure they know that rowing hard together to the destination is the price of admission... and if he doesn't want to do that, then you're better off without your other guys having to row for him – especially if he is going to likely throw mud into their ears! Anyway, faith comes from hearing the message. So now you know nearly the whole handful... SEE it, SAY it, START it, then SHARE it with others and build your team!"

Matthew grinned. "Thanks coach – I'll SHARE with the guys... and everyone else I see!"

"Good, Matthew. That's all I had to share today. You can go if you want."

"Sounds good, coach. See you tomorrow!" And Matthew left.

CHAPTER 14

SHARING IS CARING

MATTHEW'S HOMEROOM TEACHER FELT HER jaw drop when she saw him. He walked into school wearing faded jeans, but instead of his normal hooded school sweatshirt he wore a t-shirt that would surprise more than just his homeroom teacher and peers.

It was a topic of conversation by most of the student body by lunchtime, and every time somebody read it, or mentioned it in a conversation he overheard, he smiled.

By the end of the day, nearly all of his teammates had found him and commented on it as well – mostly just about how hilarious it was – and not one of them was against it. But when Matthew reached the locker room after school to get ready for their early practice, he was shocked to see Peter walking towards him, eyes and lips curled into a snarl.

"Are you serious? What were you thinking, wearing that thing to school?"

Matthew wasn't sure how to react. "It was supposed to be funny, Pete. Get people to pay attention to what we're doing, and support us a little more."

"Oh, what's funny is, that," he pointed, "makes you look like a fool."

The 'that' he referred to was a plain white t-shirt with an identical purple sharpie message written in capital letters on both the front and back, in Matthew's handwriting. Both sides read "Hebrews Basketball – If we don't make state, we'll eat live bait!"

"It's a shirt, man," said Luke.

"So are YOU gonna eat live bait? Worms? Minnows? Cause I'm not! I didn't sign up for that when I made the team."

"No worries, Pete. You won't have to do that... We just need to make state, buddy!"

Coach Carpenter walked in, and looked at Matthew. "Heard about the shirt, Matthew. Great idea... guess everybody on campus knows where you're going, right?"

"Straight to state, coach" he smiled.

Pete went to his locker to finish dressing out for practice, and nothing more was said, but it was clear that he didn't yet believe.

Monday's practice was exhausting, upbeat, and went by quickly. They spent a good bit of time preparing for Greene County's zone defense. When they were done, Coach Carpenter called them to a sideline for a few announcements.

"Okay guys. A couple of things to share with you... First, Coach Dudley contacted the principal this morning, and his brother passed away yesterday. He will be returning after the funeral to take over again. I just want to remind you to appreciate your family and make sure they know you care about them. You never know when someone on your team – and we are family – will be called back home. Second, because it's a home game, I'll see you here no later than 6:00pm. Make sure you eat something, and keep your mind on how to beat that match-up zone you're going to see. Got it?"

"Yes, sir!" Then they raised their hands high together. "One, two, three – make state!"

Pete's voice was faint at best when they did this, Matthew noticed, and he wanted to do something to connect with Pete and help him get more invested in their journey.

He knew from their teammate background discussion over a week ago that Pete lived with his dad only, just like Matthew. But Pete had a little brother, and his dad made pretty good money working with an investment company, so they had a lot less in common when it came to finances.

Matthew decided to talk to him Tuesday morning, and just before lunch invited him to hang out after school and watch some game video – but this attempt was denied also.

Confused and a little disappointed, Matthew went to see the janitor in the coach's office.

"Hey, Coach. I've got a problem"

"Okay. Tell me about it." He motioned for Matthew to sit down.

"Well, it's really about a teammate. I've asked Pete three times now to get together and watch game film. It worked great with Keith and Luke, but he just refuses to come. Says he has too much to do. I just don't know if he's all here, you know? Out of our whole team, he's the one I worry about not completely buying in..."

"Well, I think it's terrific that you've started spending the time watching film with some of your teammates. I also don't know if you saw them, but this morning Luke and Simon came in and got up about 200 shots before school."

Matthew smiled, pleased to hear that, but it wasn't what he was most concerned about.

"As far as Pete goes – you need to realize that everybody is fighting their own private battles in life, and you won't always know what those are, even when you think you know a lot about them. Pete shared some of his situation with you guys, but it wasn't the whole story. His dad doesn't want him to play."

He waited for Matthew to understand what he was saying.

"Pete's being pulled in two different directions, and while he wants to be part of this team, his dad tells him it's a waste of time and he should be helping watch his younger brother and spending more time preparing for college. From what I can see, Pete probably wants to be able to show up more often and work on his skills, or watch game tape, but it just isn't something he's allowed to do right now."

Matthew tried to imagine being in Pete's shoes.

"So what do I do?"

"Well, just like you get a little embarrassed about your dad's apathy, I would expect that Pete may be upset by – embarrassed – by his dad's disdain for something his son truly cares about. You never know how people will handle their internal hurts, Matthew."

"You know, coach, I guess I have always poured myself into working harder and spending more time in the gym... mostly because I didn't feel like I was good enough and wanted to make sure that I showed people that I could be good at something. Maybe Pete just turned his hurt the other way. Maybe it hurts him more every time I ask him to do something he knows his dad wouldn't allow."

"You're a smart kid, Matthew."

The janitor leaned back in his chair, proud of the insight Matthew had exhibited.

"So what do I do?" he repeated, sincerely troubled.

"It's like I said earlier. You love him where he is, and hold him to our standards while he's here, just like anyone else. Situations are not excuses. But you should let him know that he's important, and give him a chance to feel his contributions are appreciated."

"You think that's it?"

"Everybody on a team will have a different role. Not all actors can play the lead. But if all of the cast, even the actors with small parts, can feel included in the show's success, then you have a good show."

Matthew exhaled long and loud.

"Alright, then. I'll catch him doing something right."

He lifted his body out of the chair and thanked coach for his advice, still not completely convinced that love could solve all the team's problems, but willing to give it a try in Pete's case, at least.

CHAPTER 15

STORMY WEATHER

DURING THE GAME, MATTHEW SHARED energetic encouragements with all his teammates, and many of them did the same with each other, but he made sure to heap an extra scoop of praise on Pete when he saw him working hard on defense or giving positive reminders to other players on the floor.

They had found hole after hole in the Greene County match-up zone when they executed what they had practiced, and the win improved their record to 5-9.

Since it was a home game, and since it fell on the day after Matthew's t-shirt stunt, there was a nice crowd there to witness and celebrate the victory from the stands.

The next morning, coach had doughnuts for them to celebrate. Practice Wednesday would be early again, right after school, and they all were looking for-ward to the chance to get back on the court together and keep improving.

But while the players were pleased to have won the game, they didn't focus on it. They were thinking of their destination, instead of looking backward.

Coach told them to meet with him in the locker room before practice. There were no chairs arranged in a circle this time, though. It was just going to be a short series of updates and reminders before they went back to work.

"Okay, guys... come over here." He had them gather on each side of a row of lockers.

"First, I wanted to say how glad I am to see you move on from last night. Watching you in the hallways, while you should be pleased to have won last night, it didn't seem like you were focused on that. I just wanted to say good job for realizing that our journey doesn't end with beating Greene County. Think next play. It's the most important one."

And that's not all... I have some good news. Thanks to Matthew's t-shirt stunt, Jimbo's bait shop contacted the school, and has agreed to sponsor our team. They will put up an advertising banner in the gym hanging next to his shirt, if he donates it, and in return they will be picking up the bill for us to enjoy a pre-game meal the rest of the season."

Matthew felt a pat on his back from Phillip, who sat beside him, and saw Tommy smiling as he gave Paul an elbow and said "Alright!" He was always happy to eat, and his size was a testament to his enjoyment of that activity.

"One last thing" coach said. He took a deep breath.

"Coach Dudley will be returning on Monday. Please keep your thoughts and prayers with him as he is must be going through a difficult time having to bury his brother. I know he's missed you guys, and is looking forward to getting back here. So... let's have a good practice today and get ready for our next test. We've got Stapleton here on Friday."

Both the day's practice and the following were full of energy and the gym echoed with voices that reminded, encouraged, and praised good effort and attention to detail.

By Friday, Matthew felt that Pete had grown a bit more involved, too. He was smiling and talking on defense and seemed to have responded to the few extra comments that Matthew had shared when he did well, and bounced back with more intensity and less pouting when coach had him repeat a drill that he had started to go through at half speed.

The pre-game meal was a bag full of Philly Cheesesteak sandwiches, and was served in the locker room, individually wrapped in foil from the restaurant along with an assortment of chips and three gallons of lemonade.

The lemonade was thick and sweet, marinating Matthew's tongue with a tart syrupy aftertaste that stayed with him even during the game. It was a pleasant sweetness, and he had savored every bite of the cheese-drenched thinly sliced beef and sandwich roll, thankful beyond his teammates' understanding for the best food he had tasted in days.

Like the positive momentum his team was enjoying, this, too, he thought, was a result of his turning the custodian's words into action.

It was a close one, with Stapleton running their motion offense for what seemed like days before taking a shot. They held the ball and waited for Matthew's team to make a mistake, but Tommy and Paul and Phillip and Luke and Simon and even Pete came in and were solid defenders for most every possession.

It was a low-scoring game, but Hebrews pulled it out with clutch free throws when Stapleton started to foul at the end.

They were now at 6-9 heading into Saturday, and left the locker room with a real sense of togetherness and purpose. They were going to make a real run at state!

Game day shoot-around was scheduled for 10:00am, as usual, and Matthew got a ride home with Mark's Gramma when she insisted that he should not walk in the icy rain that had begun to fall. It was very nice of her, and he felt bad for them to see what came next.

His dad was sitting outside the apartment building, waiting for them, with a bottle in his hand. He got up and stumbled to the car to grab Matthew's bag when he got out.

"In the house, Matthew!"

Matthew looked back apologetically to Mark. "Thanks, Ms. Simpson. Sorry for…"

"Now, son!" His father yelled.

"See you in the morning, Mark." He muttered, and went inside to the less-public shame of his apartment.

His dad followed closely behind him, and was in a

fit of anger that he just wanted to direct at somebody else. Matthew was a convenient target. His dad had been laid off.

There would be no guaranteed income after the check that he threw onto the kitchen table was cashed. He huffed and roared about cheap labor and fat management for a while, and then the whisky took more effect and he sat down on the couch and mumbled a few minutes more before passing out with the History Channel playing on the television in front of him.

Matthew had seen this kind of anger blow up out of him before, not long after his mother had died. It was a volcanic explosion of frustration and regret that his dad was still trying to put a cap on – Matthew knew that – but it didn't make it any easier to watch or listen to.

The next morning he got to school well before the 10:00am shoot-around. He didn't want to be around to hear his dad share a shameful apology, or concoct some weak attempt at a story to convince him that this let down could lead to something better.

He was surprised to see the gym lights were on. No need to go around back and sneak in early to wait on coach or his teammates. He went in the main doors and stepped into the gym with a smile.

"Up bright and early, huh Coach Carpenter?"

"Wrong coach," Dudley's voice yelled back.

Matthew stared at the barrel-chested older man moving across the gym floor, pushing the ball rack to its familiar position at the far baseline. Coach Dudley was back, and he didn't see the custodian anywhere.

"He poked his head in a little while ago, but I told him I didn't need him around. I got back late last night and figured the best way to get over a loss is to stop thinking about it – only way to do that is to get busy with something else."

He left the balls and went to set up the clock controls at the scorer's table.

"So here I am… it was a tough three weeks, and we don't have much time left to get you guys ready for Creekwood. But I'll go through all that when the others get here, Matthew. Right now, grab a ball and shoot around for a bit – we'll get everybody back to business soon enough."

Matthew didn't know how to respond. He wanted to talk with the janitor. Not just about basketball, but about his dad and the team and his little finger.

On the way to school, the one thing that had been on his mind more than anything was a curiosity about what that last finger of his FIST was supposed to represent.

CHAPTER 16

CAPTAIN OF THE SHIP

SATURDAY MORNING FELT LIKE BEING FORCED to revisit a bad dream.

It started off well enough, with guys coming in and setting up to take free throws together with the paired routine Coach Carpenter had demanded. Rather quickly, though, with one small individual action to test Coach Dudley's reaction after another, the players seemed to incrementally lower their focus, intensity, and attention to detail that had made things so much more fun and productive the previous week.

First, Paul had started dribbling while Tommy took shots beside him. Next, when that wasn't addressed, he completely separated himself from the free throw activity and went over to the sideline to talk with Bart, who had shown up late but received no consequence for making his teammates wait on him.

It was a progression of small things that soon became more obvious ones, but before long there were twelve guys doing twelve different things and most of them with no energy or intentional desire to improve. They were back to wasting time.

Coach Dudley explained to them that the janitor who had been babysitting them in his absence was gone, and now that he was back things would be returning to "the Norm"! He then ran them through the set plays over and over, and one group stood and watched – or had separate conversations – while the other halfheartedly reviewed the cuts, screens, and passes they already knew. Instead of forcing perfection, though, Dudley seemed pleased to be back in his sideline chair at midcourt blowing a whistle and criticizing their efforts.

"Wow, you look horrible. I don't know how you won last night playing like this…"

Matthew cringed at Dudley's tone even more than the team's lowered expectations. Could the morale and vision and focus they had built really evaporate this quickly?

"Alright, then. That's enough of my morning watching this! We're done. And don't show up with this kind of energy tonight – you'll make me wonder why I came back." He chuckled after that last part, trying unsuccessfully to suggest it was only a joke.

Dudley reminded them of the game time that night, and then turned toward his office.

Luke had to call some of the guys back to huddle together and break practice – and the "one, two, three… make state" sounded like a sad imitation of the enthusiastic cheers from the night before.

When Saturday evening arrived, Matthew met his teammates outside the gym for the bus, excited to learn what pre-game meal might be provided for them. He was not the only one disappointed to learn that nothing would be served. Coach Dudley spoke to them after they were settled on the bus.

"Matthew, I heard about your stunt. The owner of Jimbo's called earlier today. I told him you might be going to his place for a bucket of minnows at the end of the season, but he could keep his meals for now. We need to stay hungry for a win, not show up fat and happy. Right guys?"

He looked for agreement from Paul, who hesitated before nodding.

"So let's go get those Creekwood Chiefs! We're here to win a basketball game!"

There was a muffled roar of agreement, and then everyone isolated themselves by giving their attention to music or a cell phone. It was a silent ride, and the locker room was flat before game time as they got their uniforms on. Still, when the clock started they were effective enough to win. They took an early lead and while they were obviously sloppy and less vocal with one another, by the end of the game they were still up by ten and Coach Dudley was a much happier man.

"That's what I'm talking about! It's all about getting the win, fellas. We can enjoy the rest of the weekend and we'll talk about our next game at practice Monday. I think we practice late."

He beamed with pride at the impact he felt his return had made on the team.

"Got you fellas back on the road to respectability – almost .500! Tell ya what – I saw most of your parents here – how 'bout you go home with them if they want to take you out for a bite? If not, the bus leaves in five!"

Matthew was one of the few that rode the bus back home, and was starving when he finally left the school to go home and maybe make a sandwich.

When Monday arrived, the first thing Matthew wanted to do was find the janitor.

He went hall to hall through the school searching before homeroom, and after grabbing a lunch tray went down to the gym, hoping to see him in there or around the coaching office.

There was no sign of him.

While down at the office, he saw Coach Dudley and peeked in to let him know about the film work that he had set up with players before late practice began. "I've already talked to Simon, and we just need to borrow the video cart to watch film after school. That be okay?"

Dudley looked uncomfortable. "Film work? I think that's a bit much, Matthew. We just won, remember? How about you just hang on and wait for practice. You guys just focus on playing and we'll be fine."

Matthew couldn't believe it.

"Um... well, okay... I'll just tell him just to be here for practice, then."

"Good. See you then." And Coach Dudley turned his attention back to the newspaper on his desk. By the time school had ended, Matthew was even more concerned about the janitor. After the final bell to release them, he went to the main office to find out what he could.

He found Principal Meeks outside the office and on his way to the busses for supervision.

"Principal Meeks," he said, politely, "I can't find Mr. Carpenter. I looked for him all day, and he's not been here. Do you know if he's okay?"

Meeks motioned for Matthew to walk with him as he briskly moved in the direction of the bus lane.

"Funny you should ask. He was actually in my office this morning when I got an email about the need for a head janitor up in Farrow County. He took the day off to go up there for an interview."

"Oh..."

"Glad to have Coach Dudley back?"

"I guess. But Coach Carpenter was good."

"Okay – well, good luck the rest of the year."

"Yes, sir. Thanks..." and Matthew went to wait in the locker room by himself.

CHAPTER 17

RESULTS AND REMINDERS

PRACTICE MONDAY EVENING WAS A frustrating mix of negative comments by Coach Dudley and the apathetic repetition of poor habits by his teammates. Matthew continued to yell out encouragement and give the energy he knew they needed, but without the support of his coach he felt powerless.

He talked a little about it with Phillip after practice ended, and asked if he really thought they were still focused on making state.

"I don't know, man. Seems like the airs gone out of our sails or something. I know what you mean, but who knows what we can do about it, right?" Phillip shrugged and went to catch his ride.

There were still seven people who showed up for game-day morning skill work, even though Coach Dudley hadn't required it. Matthew saw that as a good sign, but was displeased that a few had not chosen to attend. They needed to do this together.

Matthew woke early again Tuesday and got his bag of equipment and clothes prepared. His dad was still sleeping on the couch after finishing off a twelve-pack the night before. Matthew turned off the television and closed the door behind him, then arrived at the gym for game-day shoot-around stuff at 6:45am.

He was the first person there, which wasn't unusual, but was only joined by three other teammates before the 8:00am bell sounded to send them into the locker room to change and get dressed for classes. He, Tommy, Matthew, and Simon were there – and he was glad to see Simon spending the extra time working on his outside shot with such enthusiasm.

As they were changing, Matthew looked past his disappointment with those who had not shown up and chose to applaud the ones who had been there for their dedication.

"I appreciate you guys being here this morning. We need to get the others to start coming again and have everybody here together, but it is great to have you guys still putting in the time. Simon, your shot is looking good – I think you drained 4 or 5 in a row from the corner!"

Simon responded with excitement. "Yeah, my uncle keeps telling me I need to get a few hundred shots up if I wanted to get better. He says I need to be more aggressive – he's gonna give me fifty bucks for every three-pointer I made the rest of the year! If I make three or four each game, I'll be able to get that truck my neighbor is selling!"

Matthew's mouth straightened from a smile to a look of concern. That didn't sound like it was the best thing for the team ... but he finished getting dressed and went through the rest of his day.

He hoped everything would continue to go well at tonight's game like it had over the weekend on both Friday and Saturday. This was the first game of February, and began their stretch run to establish the regional playoff seeding, and at 7-9, they needed to get every win they could to improve their position in the region standings and make it into one of the top four spots.

Unfortunately, the Hamilton game Tuesday night was not their best effort.

Coach Dudley called two timeouts the first five minutes of the game, and yelled at them in the huddle for the lack of intensity and individual plays. Simon had broken the flow of their offense three times already to take shots that were either contested or off-balance, and nobody was talking on defense or blocking out consistently.

At halftime, the team sat through another barrage of criticisms – but Matthew could tell that before Dudley had gotten halfway through his list of mistakes that needed to be corrected, the team had begun to shut his voice out and nod without really listening. Paul seemed to roll his eyes to emphasize his renegade status at just about every pause.

The third quarter saw Hamilton take a twenty point lead, and by the fourth quarter they were coasting along with their home fans getting louder and more arrogant, and their bench players getting mop-up experience for the final five minutes.

Matthew's team had slid back into playing like a group of individuals, and he knew that something needed to be done if their season was going to end well – the way he thought it might just a few days earlier.

But he had already stood up and spoken to his teammates. He had taken the Custodian's advice and had been willing to SEE, and SAY, and START, and then SHARE like he had suggested. He had stood up to Paul and insisted they buy into playing for each other and a goal larger than themselves.

And now, with Carpenter missing and Dudley back in charge, it seemed that the program was slipping back into its familiar rut of mediocrity and frustration.

Oakmont High was waiting as their next home game on Friday, and Matthew had no idea what he should do to right the ship. But he knew the next couple of days at practice would be important, and he wanted to get his team back on the same page.

When he got home, his father was still awake – and didn't even ask about how the game had gone. He was wrapped up in his own situation and whether it was pain, shame, or anger that caused it, he was also slipping further away into a cloud of depression.

Matthew got a shower and went straight back to his bed without a word said between them.

CHAPTER 18

DON'T LOSE THE LESSON

THE HEBREWS KNIGHTS WERE 7-10, AND that Wednesday morning Matthew made it to the gym before 7:00am, and this time was not at all surprised to have the majority of his teammates not show up for the extra morning work and camaraderie he had tried to organize.

He learned that coach Dudley had called in sick and taken the day off. That was fine with Matthew, and gave him the chance to grab his tray during lunch and go down to the coach's office to watch film from their first game at Oakmont.

They had lost at home in the first game of the season, and he wanted to take another look at the offense they ran and the tendencies their left-handed point guard had shown.

He was surprised to see someone moving around in the coach's office when he got there with his tray of food, and even more surprised when he got a few steps closer and saw that it was Coach Carpenter in the office gathering a few things into a box.

Matthew still held his tray in one hand while the other opened the office door. "Where have you been, Coach?"

"Hi, Matthew. It's good you came down here so we could talk."

He sat down and motioned for Matthew to do the same. "I've been called to help take care of a school in another system, and with Dudley coming back, it seemed the right time to accept another opportunity there."

Matthew grabbed a fry from the tray, and said nothing, waiting for the custodian to continue.

"So you guys had a rough one last night, I hear."

"Yeah – it was brutal. It's just not the same without you here for us."

Again, Carpenter smiled and looked warmly at Matthew, the way he had that first night weeks ago.

"You know, no matter what your record is or what you've done in the past, you can still get to the Promised Land if you want to."

"I'm not so sure. Coach Dudley is just different. The guys don't play as hard for him. And we've got players playing for themselves instead of the team. Things are just falling apart."

Matthew shook his head and grabbed another fry. "I really don't have any idea what Friday's game against Oakmont will be like – but I'd be willing to bet it isn't going to be pretty with Dudley leading us."

"That may be true. I think you may be right about that."

Matthew didn't expect him to agree. He was supposed to be encouraging and positive, right?

"Huh?"

"If Coach Dudley was the only one to lead your team, it probably wouldn't be pretty. But I don't recall any of our past conversations focusing on someone else's leadership. From what I remember we always spoke about what you could do to influence others. Coach Dudley isn't the problem. Your teammates are not the problem. YOU are the problem."

"Me? I've been working harder than anybody!"

"Yes, you have. And you have had a strong impact on your teammates, too, because of it. But you can't control anyone other than yourself. You must take ownership and claim responsibility for what happens on your team. And by holding yourself accountable, you give others the example and inspiration to do the same. That is what builds a great team, Matthew. It isn't your coach that is responsible for what you accomplish – it is you."

"Then why do we even need a coach?"

"Because not everyone is as strong or disciplined as they should be for as long as they should be. Sometimes people need to be pushed, nudged, challenged, or encouraged to be and do more than they would have without another person demanding it of them."

Matthew leaned over to grab his carton of chocolate milk, and seemed to be holding back from saying something to argue the point, but remained silent and took a drink, eyes on the janitor.

"Matthew, the power of any church isn't the preacher or pulpit. The power of a church is found in its pews. It is the people that decide to take action and make their lives a small contributing part of something greater than themselves. Your coach or boss or preacher can't keep you inside walls that you aren't willing to accept. If you want to lead, from any position in an organization, it is your vision and actions that will build a following. Positions don't lead. People do."

This made Matthew think. He had led his team into a different attitude and some better habits and expectations, but still, that was different. That was with Coach Carpenter here to feed him the advice that he needed.

"I know that, too, Matthew."

Matthew looked up at the custodian. "What?"

"I know that you will need guidance. That is why, when I suggested that you needed to start something. In addition to building the fundamentals that would allow you to succeed, I also advised that you start spending some quiet time alone with the best book you could find. Start to work harder and seek wisdom, remember that?"

"Yes, sir."

"Well, this is the last lesson I have for you before I leave. You are on the right path, now you must be willing to overcome the difficulties and stay on that path. You will be tempted by convenience, by distractions, by criticism, and by doubt – but the last finger in the fist we've talked about is that you must STAY committed to what you began. Nothing great is achieved without persever-ance, and your willingness to push through the adversities you face is completely determined by the faith you have that your goal is worthwhile."

"SEE IT, SAY IT, START IT, SHARE IT, STAY IT?"

"That's right, Matthew! Some people get over a speed bump or two and start moving in the right direc-tion... but when they get to the first stop sign, they are ready to get out of the car and quit or go home... you have to let the team you are leading know that there will be stop signs on the road to success – maybe even a de-tour – but if they want what's at the end badly enough, they'll keep driving and stay on the road – no matter how inconvenient the wait!

That's your last finger, Matthew – the one that re-minds you to stay on course ... to persevere ... and as small as that finger is, it may be the most important, because without it all others are useless ... you must be willing to stay tough and keep working through adver-sity! Keep doing what you know is right the right way, and the rewards and harvest will come!"

"Even when we lose and my teammates talk about quitting? How can I stay up then?"

Coach Carpenter rose up from the desk before speaking. "Matthew, obstacles are sometimes put there to test us, to see how badly we want to fight for what lies behind them. When you try anything difficult, you will have to fail a few times before you become ready to achieve it.

"Matthew, you may lose at times, but you should never lose the lesson it offers. Do you have any idea what the letters/in the word FIST mean?"

"I never thought about it."

Carpenter grabbed his box, added a couple of files from off the desk, and moved toward the office door to leave. "From now on, making a fist will remind you that Failure Inspires Successful Toughness. Now I won't be here for a while – but you can be sure that I am paying attention and keeping an eye on you and the leadership you provide your teammates."

Matthew looked down at his school-made Sloppy Joe and frozen peaches that hadn't yet been touched. It had to be nearly the end of his lunch period.

"Leadership is not position. It's passion. Lead from where you are, Matthew"

And with that last thought, he nodded and walked out of the office, leaving Matthew with his lunch, his thoughts, and a few minutes to watch the DVD of Oakmont that Carpenter had left sitting on the desk for him.

Wednesday afternoon saw Dudley return to run practice, and it turned out to be almost exactly what Matthew anticipated it would – but he didn't let Dudley's criticisms or sarcastic remarks dull his enthusiasm or passion for what he intended to inspire his team to accomplish.

Practice was much less structured that afternoon, and the team was less than inspired by Coach Dudley's growling remarks – but Matthew could tell that his energy and effort and encouragements were being noticed. "One man, with passion, is a majority" – is what his English teacher had said when quoting somebody a few days ago, and after speaking with Coach Carpenter, Matthew was beginning to understand exactly what that quote meant.

He was going to live the quote and make-it reality here at Hebrews.

On Thursday Matthew wore his "Make State or Eat Bait" shirt again.

And Friday night, against Oakmont, the guys played three very good quarters of basketball, but when things got tough down the stretch they played as individuals and tried to do too much on their own offensively. They took bad shots and played a very sloppy fourth quarter that lived down to the comments Coach Dudley had made about their poor defense and selfishness.

The final score was Hebrews 66, Oakmont 62. The home crowd, even in victory, had been silenced by Oakmont fans who had seen their team rally back and almost pull out an unlikely win.

Matthew's teammates dragged their feet back to the locker room, many with towels covering their faces in disgust at the way they had finished the game.

It was a win, but it hadn't felt very good. The Knights were now 8-10 with only two regular season games left before the region playoffs.

They were in the fifth spot, behind Oakmont, Milford, Thompson, and Roman Hills, and needed desperately to win their last two.

After Dudley had given his post-mortem and announced their noon pregame walkthrough, and after his teammates had cleared out, Matthew found himself alone in the locker room with his hands on his forehead and sweat dripping onto the concrete floor in a too-familiar moment of frustration.

It was after Coach Dudley yelled in that he was locking up in ten minutes that Matthew did something that changed his life. He gritted his teeth, clenched his fists, took a deep breath, and then began to shake his clenched right fist slowly in the air.

CHAPTER 19

ROWING TOGETHER

SATURDAY BROUGHT WITH IT THE MAKE-UP game from the earlier cancelled game with Thompson High, from when Coach Dudley had first been called away briefly for the illness in his family.

Matthew had called Tommy early Saturday morning, and together they called every player on the team and organized a players-only meeting for 11:00am. – an hour before practice would start.

At 7:30am Matthew was having an awkward breakfast with his dad. His dad looked hung over and tired, but said he was intent on spending a few minutes with his son.

"Season okay so far?" His dad made them both a glass of water from the sink to wash the pancakes down, and put both on the table while he waited for his son to respond.

"Yeah. We're doing okay."

"Think I might come see you play your next home game. I haven't been able to watch you with the job hunting and all."

He caught himself. "Guess I haven't been much good to anybody for a while."

Matthew kept chewing.

"You know, I found out yesterday there might be a few spots coming open next week with a crew that does commercial work."

"Mm hmm."

"How are your grades – still where they're supposed to be?"

"Yeah – Yes, sir."

"Good."

Matthew took the last bite and looked toward the clock on the wall.

"Well. Good, then. You need to leave?"

"We got practice."

His dad sighed, unsure what he could say to his son that might possibly express his feelings.

"Well. Go on, then. Make us proud."

That last part escaped his mouth before he could correct himself.

It was what he used to say when mom was alive. "Make us proud." It was probably why Matthew worked so hard at basketball, and grades and staying out of trouble. If she wasn't here, he hoped she was watching from above. Matthew hoped that he was still making her proud.

His dad was a different story. His dad was trying,

he guessed, in his own sad stubborn way. He just did not seem to be trying hard enough to make anyone proud.

Matthew made it to the gym by 9:30, and spent the next hour and a half working on what he wanted to say and how he needed to say it to the teammates he knew he needed to depend on to succeed.

When 11:00am finally arrived, his emotions had his stomach twisted and aching a little – maybe that was the pancakes – but he refused to let that keep him from saying what needed to be said. He waited until the last of his teammates arrived – it was Paul, of course, who strolled in about five minutes late – and then Matthew stood up to deliver his message to them all.

"Just over two weeks ago I talked to you guys and tried to get everybody together and committed to accomplishing the same goal. That's when we started to break our huddles with 'Make State,' and that made us focus and work hard for a while. But then we had a bad game, then another, and instead of sticking together and staying committed, we had guys who chose to jump off the ship." He looked at Paul for a brief second longer than the others and paused on that point.

"Instead of rowing harder, or trying to plug the holes, we have guys who dropped their oars or started rowing for themselves in a different direction. But you can't get where we want to go without staying on course and fighting through a storm or two."

Matthew felt more comfortable now than he had anticipated. The words were flowing out of him, and he felt a power surging in his belly that inspired each syllable as it was delivered.

"I know about storms. I'm in the middle of one at home ... and you guys know about my mom already ... but the only way to get through a storm is to keep moving ahead. If you stop to pout or complain or blame someone else, you just stay in the middle' of it. That's where we are right now we're in the middle of it. This is our season."

He pointed in the direction of the poster they had signed a long time ago. Matthew saw Paul start to lean over and whisper to James, who was sitting beside him on the concrete bench.

Paul was just startled enough to let him.

"This is our season. And that sign was a promise we made. To ourselves and to each other. And I keep my promises!"

Keith nodded his head and looked around the locker room to see who else was willing to join him.

"I keep my promises. And I take full responsibility for keeping them. I am here today because I intend to keep them. And I need your help. My mom used to tell me to dream big dreams that required great teams. So I need your help to keep my promise."

He looked again at Paul.

Luke nodded.

"Luke – remember when we talked about SEEING where we wanted to go together? Remember the smell of Tech's gym? Can you still see us there playing in the tournament in front of all those people? Can you still hear them screaming and cheering as we take the floor for warm-ups?"

"And Tommy, remember how much harder we worked when we told ourselves we were going to Make State? When we kept SAYING what we wanted to make happen instead of listening to doubts or criticisms of others?"

Tommy poked out his lower lip and rocked forward and back in agreement.

"And Keith, do you remember STARTING those film sessions after school? Don't all you guys remember how great it felt to get in here together in the mornings when we started those extra shoot-arounds when it was just us and we woke up and worked for each other'!"

Most of the team had joined in and was nodding in rhythm with each of his points.

"And Paul – remember how it felt to know that people were watching us and waiting to see how we did the game after I wore that State or Bait t-shirt? Remember how SHARING our goal with others made it a challenge for us to do what others thought was too difficult?"

Instead of smirking or eye rolling, Paul seemed sincerely thoughtful.

"Guys – I intend to keep the promise I made. But I need your help. I need you guys to keep rowing with me no matter how bad the storm gets, no matter how many shots we miss, no matter how many people say you should just give up. We need to commit to STAYING on the course we set and focus on what the team needs instead of playing for ourselves. We need to stick together and keep working and do the right things the right way for as long as it takes to get where we want to go!"

"Yeah!" came out, almost uncontrollably, from James' mouth. The whole team was enthralled and growing increasingly inspired by Matthew's speech.

"And WE decide where we end up! No more caring about who gets credit for it, no more playing like individuals, no more being discouraged by the obstacles that are put in our way – WE stay together and keep rowing through the storm, because WE decide how and where the season ends!

We will play loud, and we will play hard, and we will keep the promise and Make State!"

"Let's do this thing!" yelled Simon. And they crashed together into a tight knot of bodies and high fives of enthusiasm, and just before noon arrived they decide to slap the poster they had signed every day for the rest of the year to remind themselves of the promises they would keep.

At the pregame shoot-around, Coach Dudley called everyone together to blame the last two losses on his absence. "That's where the blame goes, fellas...," he said, "take time away and this is what I get. You can't be expected to coach yourselves, right? But we're getting ready for Thompson tonight. We're getting back to the Norm!"

Some of the players smirked, some nodded politely, but they all went into that practice inspired not by

Dudley, but by Matthew, Tommy and Paul and the passion they showed. Every oar was in the water and moving in unison throughout the 90 minute practice session. Even Paul and Tommy seemed willing to do what everyone else expected – play loud and play hard.

Matthew felt better – they acted like they were back on the same page again and finally refocused on the goal of working together to make state.

Coach Dudley finished the practice session with a new inbounds play he wanted to run for Keith to get an inside touch or for Simon to get an open shot if Keith was doubled. Everyone gathered together after Coach Dudley had them all make 20 free throws.

In the huddle to end practice they were focused and sincere and louder than ever when they broke it, saying "Make State!"

CHAPTER 20

TOUGHNESS WINS

TOUGHNESS IS BEST ILLUSTRATED BY consistency, and the Hebrews basketball team began to show that they had become tougher than ever as they gave two strong efforts where they looked and played better than they had all year.

After losing to Oakmont, the Knights beat Thompson on Saturday by eight, and then continued to play inspired basketball together as they finished up their regular season schedule by beating Loganville convincingly, 62-46.

Matthew's dad had not been at either of them, but Matthew and his teammates refused to be distracted or discouraged by anything – whether family, friends, or referees. They dove on the floor, passed up good shots for great ones, blocked out, and grew hoarse from encouraging each other.

Coach Dudley was happy to take the credit for the resulting wins, and was confident that his return to the team had been the only thing that could possibly have saved what was an underachieving bunch for the majority of the year. Only the guys in the locker room who had begun playing so hard for each other over the last week had any clue that the major reason for their intense and sudden decision to focus on getting results instead of recognition was the influence of a janitor who had come and gone in relative obscurity.

"Hey, man!"

That fact wasn't lost on Matthew, though, and he missed his conversations with Coach Carpenter, often wondering where he was and who he might be inspiring wisdom now.

It was the middle of February, and the team was 10-10. They had taken over the fourth place in their region to make the playoffs.

Milford was waiting as their opponent on Thursday. If they lost, the season would be over, but if they won they would play Saturday for the region championship and a chance to go to State against the winner of Roman Hills and Oakmont.

Wednesday afternoon's practice was late, from 6-8 in the evening, and Matthew stayed at the school to take care of grades and just be in the locker room with whichever guys stayed instead of going I home and coming back.

Tommy was the only one in the locker room when Matthew got there after going for a few minutes of extra help in math, and Matthew was both surprised and glad to not be alone for the next few hours!

"Hey, Matthew. Pretty amazing last few days, huh. Kids in the hallways and everything."

Tommy was standing in front of his locker, bouncing a ball behind his back from his right hand to his left as he spoke.

"Yeah."

Tommy was referring to the attention they were getting going into the next couple of games that came from the t-shirt he had worn to advertise their commitment to the cause,

"Think we'll finish the job?"

"I know we will. Just gotta keep thinking about where we're going and do what the team needs from us."

Matthew grabbed a ball and sat down, dribbling figure eights around his ankles.

"So, you still on board?"

"Yeah. I talked last night with Paul, too. You know, he was our best rebounder Friday. Told me he just had something come over him on the way to school that morning."

He held the ball in front of him and finished his thought, almost talking to himself.

"Right after that, He says he just got more intense. It seems like everybody's full steam ahead with blinders on, and all they see is the region tournament."

"It's been pretty cool to feel everybody working for the same thing. I'm glad you stayed after, Tommy. Nice to not be here by myself."

"Yeah, me too. So you wanna go watch a little game tape?"

Matthew nodded and followed him to the coach's office. Dudley would be back just before six o'clock, which gave them time to look again at what Milford's press rotations were.

By 5:30, every player had gotten back to the gym and they shared a few minutes together as a team in the locker room before practice, talking about their upcoming game and who needed to do what to make sure they got to Saturday's region championship and the shot at state.

Dudley burst through the gym door at 5:52, and his hand held a practice plan scribbled in pencil.

It honestly didn't matter what he asked them to do, though – every drill, every offensive run-through was sharp and mistake free. Every player squeaked out and contested shots, called the ball, pivoted and passed strong out of pressure, and paid attention to the details that weeks ago would have been ignored.

When Thursday arrived, they cut through Milford's half-court trap with surgical precision and were up ten points by the end of the first quarter. They held the Milford big guy to only one offensive rebound, when Paul had left him to rotate over and stop a drive. It was another loud and positive team effort, and they woke up Friday morning one game away from the goal they had set.

Roman Hills had won the other semi-final region game, and they would host Hebrews on Saturday at 8:00pm with a trip to the state playoffs at stake, not to mention a meal of fish bait if Matthew let his team lose it somehow.

Practice Friday went by like a blur. Matthew spent the evening that followed home alone, and fell asleep before his dad made it home around 3:00am.

Saturday morning came, and Matthew saw him still fully clothed, half-conscious and snoring, on the couch. Sneaking out without waking him, Matthew took his equipment bag full of clothes and his game shoes. He figured it was better to spend the afternoon at the gym after 10:00am shoot-around was over.

He could rest up in the locker room or work on his ball-handling some more if he wanted to.

CHAPTER 21

LETTING OUT THE LIGHT

THE BUS RIDE TO ROMAN HILLS HIGH THAT evening was almost completely silent, except for the hum of the bus heaters and Coach Dudley talking on his phone occasionally.

Each player was either lost in his own thoughts or preparing for the game with a playlist of songs pumping through his earplugs.

The visitors' locker room was cool, and they dressed quietly as well. Then Coach Dudley came in for the pregame speech, where he talked about their classmates and the record books and making history and how seldom this moment might come along in their lives – then he left them to themselves for a moment.

"Hey, guys, huddle up."

It was Keith, and then he nodded to Matthew to take over. The team formed a circle, and Matthew spoke in a calm voice.

"Okay, team. We made it this far – might as well do what we came for."

He looked around the circle at his teammates.

"Tonight will make us 12-10, but it isn't about our record books or about our classmates. It is about us keeping our promise. Okay – let's pray."

And, just like they had for the last three games, Matthew and his teammates joined hands and said the Lord's Prayer, then raised their fists together and yelled in unison, "Make State!"

Hebrews High lead early, but Roman Hills wouldn't told and made some amazing shots to battle back and take a one point lead at halftime. Dudley was furious about the referees and blamed them for the game even being close at all, but Matthew and his teammates remained focused and refused to use that crutch. They looked around at each other, and when Dudley went out to take the floor, they reminded each other of the things they could control, like ball pressure, getting into the paint, and blocking out every time.

"Fundamentals, guys," said Tommy.

"Let's take great shots," said Simon.

And they ran out to begin the second half.

It was back and forth until the last minute of the third quarter, when Keith turned the ball over twice against a surprise full-court trap and gave up two easy layups. When Peter missed a layup at the other end after a terrific pass by Tommy, Roman Hills took the ball and heaved up a nearly half-court shot that looked like it would hit the gym ceiling.

As it came down, it barely touched anything and swished through the net for three more points, and their home crowd stood up and went wild as the horn sounded with Roman Hills leading 48-41 with only eight minutes to play.

Dudley nodded and motioned an upturned palm in the direction of the bench as assent.

When they took the floor again, Matthew stole the inbounds pass and sent it ahead to Tommy to draw them back within five points, but, even against Hebrews' good defense, Roman Hills made a couple of tough outside shots and stretched the lead to nine with about five minutes left.

On the very next trip down the floor, Simon took a quick three that he shouldn't have, and when the ball flew out of bounds off a Roman Hills player, Paul immediately called a timeout.

The players jogged over and fell back into the sideline scats and grabbed their water bottles. Even Matthew felt the urge to throw back his head and roll his eyes in frustration. Coach Dudley went over to confirm how many timeouts they had at the scorer's table, and then turned to address his team – but Paul took a last quick drag of water from his bottle, stood up, and waved him off.

"Coach ... Let me." He breathed deep. "I want to say something."

Paul went over to face the seats his team waited in, and took a knee in front of them as they made a horseshoe of bodies for the thirty seconds had had to speak.

"Four minutes and fourteen seconds. That's how long we have to make this right! I wasn't always on board, guys – but I'm here now – and I'm rowing hard – and I want you all to remember what Matthew said to us all those times before today..."

He paused to glance over at Matthew.

"We can't do it by ourselves! Everybody blocks out, everybody passes up good shots for great shots, and everybody keeps believing and encouraging each other! Right?"

"RIGHT!"

"Okay – Let's go!"

Hebrews High took the floor and scored, then got a stop and scored again, then stole a pass and scored again, then got a rebound and ran a play for Simon to get an open shot. He wasn't open, and instead of taking a bad shot, he passed it inside to Paul, who missed the layup, got his own rebound, and kicked it back outside to Simon who was open this time – and Simon made the shot.

In less than a minute they had tied the game, and Romans called their own timeout.

Coach Dudley told them that if they got the lead, they were to hold the ball and run their delay game when it got under three minutes. Roman Hills scored inside against Tommy on their next possession, but Paul kept encouraging him to "think next play!" and "get it back!" as they ran back down the floor. And it was Tommy who made a baseline jump-shot to tie it up again.

As Roman Hills was inbounding the ball, Matthew denied their point guard the ball and the inbounder, not expecting it to be a difficult pass, stepped on the line and turned the ball over.

When Hebrews scored and got another stop, Roman Hills started to panic. They took a couple of rushed shots themselves, and when Hebrews went into their delay game with just under two minutes to go, the frustration fouling gave Hebrews a chance to win it at the free throw line, Hebrews ended up winning by four.

The team celebrated together on the floor and in the locker room. Coach Dudley was smiling wider than Matthew had ever seen, and told them he was "so proud of all of you and how you played."

The bus ride home was much louder than the ride there, and Matthew's teammates were on the phone with girlfriends and parents and friends who wanted to hear about the game.

Matthew sat by himself and thought about Coach Carpenter working in obscurity and Paul stepping up to be such a strong voice for his teammates, and about how powerful the feeling of accomplishment was when you did something that required more than just your own efforts.

On Monday, Matthew wore his "State or Bait" t-shirt one last time, and that afternoon Principal Meeks visited their locker room and announced he would be purchasing rings for the team after their season finally ended – hopefully not for a few more games.

They had made state and won a region championship for the first time in school history!

CHAPTER 22

THE REWARDS
OF REBOUNDING

THE NEXT WEEK AT SCHOOL THEY WERE rock stars.

Practices were still pretty intense and focused, but there was a sense of relief and pride that contributed to the players not going quite as hard or being quite as loud as they had previously.

They were 12-10, going to play North Ridge on Friday in the State playoffs.

Matthew's dad was seldom home when Matthew got there each night, but Matthew had thrown himself into his team's preparation and continued to spend more and more time at the school in order to keep from having any kind of uncomfortable encounter.

They stayed after practice on Monday and Wednesday to watch film on North Ridge and Coach

Dudley pointed out the strengths they needed to take away, while emphasizing the best way he felt they could attack them offensively.

Everyone was happy to show up early and get shots up or work on ball-handling, but it didn't seem as concentrated or intense as the morning sessions should have been.

They were still patting themselves on the back for the promise they kept, and Matthew wondered if it was wrong to criticize what he felt might be the complacency of their success.

He didn't want to appear ungrateful for what they had done to get here, but to get past here he knew it would take more than they were doing – both physically and mentally.

He wasted the first couple of days thinking about whether he should say something or not, and then by Wednesday decided he was better off not rocking the boat. It was better that they be happy together at this point, he thought.

When Friday arrived, though, he wished he had handled it differently.

North Ridge was good. Really good.

During the game, Matthew and his teammates all looked a step slow against them on defense, and looked even sloppier on offense. Their timing and passes were just not quite where they needed to be.

By halftime, Hebrews was down eleven.

They didn't turn on each other or stop encouraging, but they just didn't have the fire or focus they needed to beat a team this good.

When the final buzzer went off, they had lost by sixteen. Matthew was walking off the floor to the locker rooms, and he saw his dad sitting up in the corner of the stands. He had shaved, and looked presentable, and clapped for his son despite the loss.

In the locker room, everyone sat down and began to quietly untie their shoes, remove their ankle braces, and change.

When Coach Dudley came in, he was very brief. "I don't care about tonight, guys. You did something special this year. Remember that."

Dudley shook his head and looked at the locker room floor. "Tough end to a good ride, guys. Get your equipment back to me next week. Bus leaves in fifteen minutes – you got a while to gather your stuff."

When Dudley left, they thought the post-game coaching comments were over.

Then Coach Carpenter walked in.

"Hello, fellas."

Every player froze and looked up to see the man whose voice they recognized.

Frowns and scowls of disappointment from their loss vanished for a split second, and then slowly returned as the team remembered the moment they were enduring.

"I understand that this doesn't feel like a moment to celebrate, but you will find in the coming years that this experience has been the one you should value greatly."

He went around the room to touch the shoulder or

pat the back of each player while he spoke.

"Fellas, people will tell you that you didn't get what you deserved this year – and that is likely true, both of this basketball season and of most every other situation you will encounter in your future. You seldom get what you deserve in this world – but you do usually get what you demand ... what you demand of yourself, and what you demand of others"

He stood still to continue.

"When I leave here tonight, I will not see any of you for a very long while, although I hope we will meet again at some point. But even though I am not with you physically, you can show others that you have known my advice and wisdom by sharing your love and mercy with one another...

I know you are upset now about this game you played tonight, but I want you to always place experiences in their proper perspective. You DID accomplish what you promised yourselves. You listened when Matthew asked you to SEE, and SAY, and START, and SHARE.

And you found a way to STAY focused on that goal to make it reality. Winning state was not your goal..."

He paused to survey the room, smiled at Paul, and continued.

"My conversations with you were not about winning state. Even if you had won tonight, it would not be the top of that hill. All that waits at the top of any hill for you are the sky, a moment of pride, and the heavens above. Here on earth there will always be more mountains – and you fellas will find the tops of many in your life – but your joy will not be found at the summit.

Your joy will be in the journey and relationships you share, and the legacy and influence you leave on others.

My conversations and advice were about making yourself better, stronger, and more responsible. You learned to depend upon more than just your prideful self, and accomplish a task more challenging than you ever could dream of attempting alone.

And you learned about building relationships – not just with me, but with each other. You have a meaningful bond with those you invest your heart and your talents in, and you have learned that both people are enriched by that experience. That is why you are here!"

"Coach Carpenter... I want to talk to you about..." Matthew tried to cut in.

"You guys will be fine. Remember that a relationship doesn't require both people be physically present. And when you meet a challenge, make another fist!"

He held a fist in front of him to emphasize this.

"This is NOT the end of a great ride, fellas – it is the beginning of one. And fellas – the five things that Matthew talked to you about – the FIST you can make to focus on and achieve your goals – it works outside the gym, too. It's not just for basketball players ... This year will be a special one for each of you if you just remember the record you earned. Remember Hebrews 12-11..."

The custodian moved toward the locker room door to leave.

"And anyone of you who truly believes in what I have taught will do what I have done, and even greater things than these with others in the future. Stay in touch, fellas."

And then he left.

The bus trip back to Hebrews High was quiet.

CHAPTER 23

RIPPLES OF INFLUENCE

MATTHEW WENT HOME CONTENT TO KNOW that other mountains waited, pleased that he had grown and learned what he had this season, and excited as he looked forward to the many opportunities he would have to apply Coach Carpenter's lessons and help influence others.

That night, oddly enough, his dad was there waiting at the kitchen table for him.

"I saw you at the game, dad."

His dad's head drooped with chin down, sobbing quietly to himself instead of answering...

"Dad, I should be mad at you right now. I could be angry and resent you for not doing so many things. But I don't think that's why we're here together. I feel like maybe I'm supposed to try and help make things better. So, what's wrong Dad?"

"Hi, Matthew." He looked up, but his hands still supported his chin, and his eyes were closed and seemed heavy with anguish. "I still don't have a job. I don't have any more credit. I don't know how I got here, son ..."

He paused a moment – and finished with what he really meant to say.

"I know I've been a terrible dad the last few months. Matthew. I'm so sorry. Guess while you moved forward I've just been feeling sorry for myself."

Matthew thought back a few months – and laughed. "Pick your head up, dad. You know, it's tough to see where you're going with your chin down."

His dad was surprised – he hadn't expected that response.

Matthew said nothing for almost a full minute while his father waited for him to continue.

Matthew's warm smile twisted somewhat into a determined scowl of intensity. He turned his once spread fingers into a clenched fist and held it up in front of himself.

Matthew then stared intently at the fist he had made, and slowly shook it.

His dad was confused and waited for an explanation.

"You're supposed to be the leader of this family, right?" asked Matthew.

His Dad replied, with some apprehension – "Yeah..."

His son's smile returned and his eyes again glowed with warmth as he held the fist in the air between them. "That's your answer, then..."

His dad didn't understand.

"Dad, this past season I learned some pretty amazing stuff. Nothing changes until you do. And it's not just wanting something that makes it happen – it's how hard and how long you are willing to work for it, especially through tough times, that really matters!"

Matthew held up his pointer finger. "Start with this. Instead of focusing on what you're going THROUGH, start choosing to focus on what you're going TO..."

CHAPTER 24

SPREADING THE WORD

THE HEBREWS HIGH BASKETBALL ATHLETES each went their separate ways, and over the next many years their bodies became thick with the food and experience that life provided.

They all carried with them and in their own way had found ways to spread the seeds of what they had learned that season – perhaps none more so than Paul.

Making his way into a high-rise office building, dressed in a nicely tailored suit with thinning hair and lines of experience on his brow, a 40 year old Paul strode into the conference room of his next corporate assignment.

His presence was met by a table of curious eyes all locked on him – the golden boy consultant who had come to turn their struggling organization into a profitable and productive one.

Paul spent the first few minutes explaining why he was hired – low sales, poor production, morale in the toilet... and department leaders' heads began to droop. As the group's chins started to drop – he paused – and then said nothing for a few moments...

Then Paul looked down at his region championship ring and smiled to himself.

He said to the board room full of management and salespeople, "The past is something we can't change. And while it's important to know where you are, it's far more important to identify where you are determined to go."

He paused a moment to scan the group – and saw some still looking at him, but many just had their chins and eyes lowered as if they were dogs being punished for soiling the floor.

Paul said, "You know, it's hard to see where you're going if your head is down," and he raised his fist to hold it beside his cheek before shaking it ever so slightly.

"That" he said, glancing suggestively at his clenched hand, "is the answer, people..." He knew it looked simplistic and clichéd to them now, but also knew from his own experience that despite the anticipated groans of cynicism, it would be the key to their future growth and success.

One of the salesmen smirked and elbowed the guy beside him, then asked Paul dryly, "Your ring is going to make us better?"

"No, not the ring." Paul smiled warmly at the salesman and remembered how cynical he, too, must have sounded so many years ago.

"While the ring is a reminder to me, it is the FIST that you need to focus on..."

And then Paul continued to address the group.

"If you want your organization to be GREAT, you have to start by identifying your island and figure out who's truly willing to be on the boat with you... "

It took a while, but eventually every one of the dozen players had found that verse that Coach Carpenter had mentioned to them before leaving.

They all, at some point, either looked for purposely or stumbled upon it in the book that became an important guide and inspiration to them all.

The twelve players from that Hebrews team traveled in very different directions after graduation, but all went on to influence thousands of people in their life, and those touched millions more with the warm words of wisdom and encouragement that had been shared first by a lowly janitor.

And each teammate realized, in his own way, the final lesson that their season had offered:

Hebrews 12:11

*"No discipline seems pleasant at the time, but painful.
Later on, however, it produces a harvest of righteousness and
peace for those who have been trained by it."*

ABOUT THE AUTHOR

SEAN GLAZE is a speaker and team building facilitator who incorporates insights from his background as a successful coach to help corporate groups, school faculties, and university athletic programs improve team performance with fun team-building events and leadership keynotes.

As an experienced author, speaker, and team-building coach, Sean entertains and influences audiences with a unique blend of engaging content, interactive activities, and practical take-aways.

His website, www.greatresultsteambuilding.com provides more information on the team-building events, keynote topics, and training workshops he offers.

If you are part of a business, school, or athletic team that needs to improve communication, energize morale, and help your people to become better teammates, contact him to discuss a customized event today!

www.ingramcontent.com/pod-product-compliance
Lightning Source LLC
Chambersburg PA
CBHW060316220326
41598CB00027B/4340